Still Hanging

Personal/Public Scholarship

VOLUME 11

The titles published in this series are listed at *brill.com/pepu*

Still Hanging

Using Performance Texts to Deconstruct Racism

By

Bryant Keith Alexander and Mary E. Weems

BRILL

SENSE

LEIDEN | BOSTON

Cover illustration: *Victims of Peonage and Vagrancy Laws*, artwork by Jerry L. Weems

All chapters in this book have undergone peer review.

The Library of Congress Cataloging-in-Publication Data is available online at http://catalog.loc.gov

Typeface for the Latin, Greek, and Cyrillic scripts: "Brill". See and download: brill.com/brill-typeface.

ISSN 2542-9671
ISBN 978-90-04-46483-4 (paperback)
ISBN 978-90-04-46484-1 (hardback)
ISBN 978-90-04-46485-8 (e-book)

This book is printed on acid-free paper and produced in a sustainable manner.

Advance Praise for
Still Hanging: Using Performance Texts to Deconstruct Racism

"In *Still Hanging,* Bryant Keith Alexander and Mary E. Weems have literally put their bodies on the line by providing readers a bird's eye view into their own personal and often painful experiences of racism. Rendered through the brilliance of their textual performances, the authors offer more than a theory of performance and instead offer performance as political praxis—as a powerful tool for recalling and calling out antiblackness. Personal, poetic, and profoundly original, *Still Hanging* deftly critiques the continual acts of racial turpitude that would have black bodies 'still hanging' in perpetuity."
– **E. Patrick Johnson, Dean, School of Communication, Northwestern University, author of** *Appropriating Blackness: Performance and the Politics of Authenticity*

"*Still Hanging* is perhaps the most deeply moving and meditative contemporary reflection on the horrific violence inflicted on Black bodies I have seen in a very long time. Although its insistent commentary on the vile history and undeniable tragedy of racism is enough to bring any of us to tears, the dynamic interplay between imagination and intellect leaves us as readers inspired and uplifted. Social justice warriors, scholar-activists, and creatives of all kinds interested in race will want to add this book to their collection."
– **Ronald L. Jackson II, author of** *Scripting the Black Masculine Body*

"*Still Hanging: Using Performance Texts to Deconstruct Racism* is a powerful, painful, and critically necessary intervention into the historical present and its inhumane legacies—ones that reverberate with systemic racism, sexism, oppression, and exploitation. At turns cathartic and therapeutic, Alexander and Weems examine through performative, poetic, and dialogic inquiry the personal, political, and performative outrages of police brutality, lynching, the Trump Era, pandemic times, and, simply, the everyday struggles to exist and live as free human beings. Their book is a masterclass in using performance texts to open up new ways of knowing and seeing each other—and the world; of being present to the horrors and hopes of our unsettled and unsettling condition. A must-read for those seeking a new collaborative framework for understanding and impacting their communities."
– **Michael Giardina, Professor, College of Education, Florida State University and Director, International Congress of Qualitative Inquiry**

"Alexander and Weems' new book, *Still Hanging: Using Performance Texts to Deconstruct Racism* is a brilliant, painful, call to arms. The title, invoking Billie Holiday's signature song, tells us that racism and genocide are alive and well in America today. Young dead black bodies, bulging eyes, twisted mouths, lie in pools of blood. The sweet smell of death everywhere, Will this ever end? Buy this book. Take action."

– **Norman Denzin, Emeritus Professor, Department of Sociology at the University of Illinois at Urbana-Champaign; Professor of Communications, Sociology, Cinema Studies, Criticism, Interpretive Theory, and Qualitative Inquiry**

*To our Black brothers and sisters, and those living in-between,
who have lost their lives due to racism and bias in America.
We stand in your place to continue the struggle.*

.:

Contents

          Mary E. Weems

      PART 3
Black/White Double Consciousness

14   Is There a White Double Consciousness? A Short Dialogue   171
          Mary E. Weems and Bryant Keith Alexander

      Study Questions, Prompts, and Probes   175
          Bryant Keith Alexander
      Notes for Teachers, Faculty, and Facilitators on Establishing a Learning
          Community   179
          Mary E. Weems
      Bibliography and Further Reading   182

Acknowledgments

We take this opportunity to sincerely thank John Bennett, Acquisitions Editor at Brill | Sense and Patricia Leavy, editor of the *Personal/Public Scholarship Series* (Brill | Sense) for their confidence in this work and for marshalling this project with their able and committed staff.

Special thanks to Judith Hamera for her continued personal and professional friendship, and her overall brilliance that inspires me always. To my brister E. Patrick Johnson, who many years ago suggested that I should engage a book project of this type—your work is consonant with my own on so many levels.

And I thank Patrick Henry Bailey for his love and on-going, level-headed support of my person and my work.

Bryant Keith Alexander

Special thanks to Nathan Motta and the Dobama Theater for inviting me to be part of its "Playwrights GYM," a group of Cleveland playwrights the theater supports with regular meetings, space for staged readings and productions, and other resources. To the Ensemble Theater, the Playwrights Local Theater Company, Karamu House, and the "Dark Room" at the Cleveland Public Theater, who provided space for staged/readings of some of this work in its early stages.

The bibliography at the end of the book was originally compiled by the late Najee Muhammad, EdD, Associate Professor, Ohio University.

I'd like to thank my husband, James Amie, for his unconditional love, patience, and unwavering support.

Mary E. Weems

Message about Cover Art

Artist: Jerry Weems

Title: "Victims of Peonage and Vagrancy Laws"

The cover image for this project is entitled "Victims of Peonage and Vagrancy Laws" by the Los Angeles-based—but Southern-born and raised—artist Jerry Weems. Peonage, also called "debt slavery" or "debt servitude," is a system where an employer compels a worker to pay off a debt with work. Legally, peonage was outlawed by Congress in 1867. Yet the Vagrancy Act of 1866, which became law shortly after the American Civil War ended in 1865, forced into employment, for terms of up to the three months, any person who appeared to be unemployed or homeless—and hence the hundreds of thousands of "African Americans" newly freed from slavery.

The law was formally in effect until 1904, but we know that peonage and the practices of vagrancy penalties lingered far longer, until the near present in the South. Hence the politics of those practices, along with the imagery of the skeletal tree with perpetually laboring Black bodies, speak to the title and theme of this project, *Still Hanging: Using Performance Texts to Deconstruct Racism.* The features of the image map upon the features of the title, which are both cultural and pedagogical: a lesson to be taught and learned, a debt to be paid and recovered one way or another.

"Still hanging" references both the resilience of Black people in the face of slavery, institutionalized racism, and systemic oppression, as well as the fact that Black people continue to be literally and metaphorically lynched in the year 2020. We are forced to pay off a debt of history's legacy of racism and resistance with our lives. The image's visual transparency of the ground, with the mirroring limbs as roots, also figuratively signifies—at least for the authors of this project—the depth of servitude and slavery, as well as the souls lost in the middle passage of slave transport. The living, consistently cultivating the graves of the ancestors.

Figures

About the Authors

Bryant Keith Alexander
(Ph.D., 1998) is Professor and Dean, College of Communication and Fine Arts, Loyola Marymount University, Los Angeles and at the time of this publication, he also serves as the Interim Dean, School of Film and Television at LMU. He is co-editor of *Performance Theories in Education: Power, Pedagogy, and the Politics of Identity* (Erlbaum, 2005); author of *Performing Black Masculinity: Race, Culture, and Queer Identity* (Alta Mira, 2006), and *The Performative Sustainability of Race: Reflections on Black Culture and the Politics of Identity* (Peter Lang, 2012); and co-editor of the *Routledge Handbook of Gender and Communication* (Routledge, 2021). Formal faculty in the Department of Communication Studies at LMU, he is also Affiliate Faculty of Educational Leadership for Social Justice, Doctoral Program at LMU's School of Education.

Mary E. Weems
(M.A., Ph.D., 2001) is an Independent Scholar, imagination-intellect theorist, poet, playwright, performer, and author of thirteen books and five chapbooks. Recent books include *Blackeyed: Plays and Monologues* (Sense, 2015) and *Writings of Healing and Resistance: Empathy and the Imagination-Intellect* (Peter Lang, 2013). She may be reached via her website at www.maryeweems.org

Introduction

The title's keywords begin to outline the critical intention and methodology of the project. "Still Hanging" serves as a double reference to the persistent history of lynching Black bodies as component residue of slavery and racial injustice in the United States of America—with an increasing number of hangings reported throughout the country in 2020, paralleling the rise of the Black Lives Matter movement. The phrase refers to the resiliency of the Black (African-American) struggle from slavery up to the current moment. The phrase was also used in the titles of various project entries to symbolize how much work we "still" have to do in the U.S. to meet the promises of freedom and democracy for all. The project as a whole uses dramatic scripts, performative, and poetic writing as the primary stylistic modality of illuminating, commenting upon, and critiquing culture focused on issues of race, racism, and social justice, while recognizing the ever-present interconnectedness and intersectionalities of sex, sexuality, and gender. Each piece draws the reader into the scene of an actual, imagined, felt, and/or remembered moment in the Black experience that is grounded in a historical truth or reality, sometimes using the author's actual and autoethnographic experiences.

Key to the project is providing a range of references, examples, and contextual frames to define and deconstruct the notion of racism. It conceives of racism as a systematic bias against people of color with material, social, political, and economic consequences—including the loss of self-esteem, livelihood, and life. The pieces in this project are designed to invoke a cultural reality and invite the reader to closely scrutinize the racial dilemmas presented. Still, they represent examples and are not monolithic to all Black peoples. The project provides poetic, prosaic, and dramatic integrative dialogue between the authors written between the movements of each text. It also includes writing prompts and reflective prompts that require the reader—the student and instructor—to deconstruct the texts. To deconstruct and analyze the texts as literary form and cultural critique is to get at the embedded and emergent meanings that are linked both to the text and context of engaging the materials and the subjects they contain for a range of instructional purposes. This is fundamental to the project.

The value of such a volume at this historical moment is that it addresses a range of issues at the confluence of: (a) challenges in national leadership that show evidence of racial, ethnic, cultural, and gender bias manifested in governmental decision-making, (b) the unregulated spread of the Coronavirus pandemic, which is disproportionately hitting communities of color with Black

© BRYANT KEITH ALEXANDER AND MARY E. WEEMS, 2021 | DOI: 10.1163/9789004464858_001

and Brown bodies at higher rates of mortality, and (c) the rise of the social, cultural, and racial activism with the Black Lives Matters movement, set-off by the repeated murders of unarmed Black people by police officers in America. These issues and their rise in this historical moment are all connected. The text provides readers, teachers, and students at all levels with a viable tool to examine and discuss pressing social and racial matters, as comparative analysis to what and how these issues are discussed in social media or the nightly news. The text is both literary and performative in style, with a critical pedagogical praxis as its grounding intention. My physical body, professional identity, and psychic reality as a Black/gay/man in America is situated between the lines of this text, both in the selections that I offer and as my sista-friend Mary narrates aspects of her lived experience. The potency, possibility, and potentiality of this volume meet at the common crossroads of our lives, both particular and plural, but equally as Black people in America.

Bryant Keith Alexander

• • •

In this messy, timely, sacred performance text, my brotha, Bryant and I continue the collaborative work we started when we co-edited "June 12, 2016: Terrorism and Hate in Orlando, America—Poetic and Performative Response," a Special Issue of *Qualitative Inquiry*.[1] As an allied Black man/woman, homo/hetero, in the academy/outside the academy, our working together creates a space to share ideas and lived experiences that intersect, connect, and disconnect. Combining our voices constructs a more powerful creative-critical union, which by existing invites others to do the same.

Like various kinds of addiction, including drugs, alcohol and food, deconstructing lifelong racist beliefs and perspectives is an individual act that takes time, hard work, and patience. This kind of change begins with each person learning and/or acknowledging that race is a social construction, a visual modifier designed to identify white people as superior and 'privileged'—and blacks and all other non-white groups as inferior—in order to justify slavery while maintaining the presumptions of white Christianity. Without this important, deeply personal revelation, it does not matter what an individual reads, sees, or is exposed to, because without being open to change, it won't happen.

This book is designed to be used in small groups in either formal classroom settings or in informal community or familial spaces, and in all cases working with an experienced teacher, educator, or facilitator. To aide this process, our book includes discussion questions, a brief guide for establishing a safe learning community, and suggested readings, films, articles, and essays to continue individual deconstructive work.

As an Imagination-Intellect theorist[2] working in interpretive methods including auto/ethnography, poetic inquiry, and ethnotheatre, empathy—or the ability to more closely identify with individuals from different race, gender, sexual orientation, and religious backgrounds—is at the heart of my work. The writings in this book reflect my continued effort to deeply connect with the experiences of all people, while honoring and loving my own Black race/ethnicity/gender/culture.

The writings I've contributed to our collaboration are grounded in my lived experience and in the lived experiences of family, friends, colleagues, and people I've never met, filtered through an informed, creative-critical, reflexive, cultural lens. As is the case with all of my work, each piece represents a political act. I share them in this context because I want to live long enough to see racism, homo/trans/binary phobia, and sexism become part of our global past. I want to live long enough to have to think long and hard to remember the last time an innocent Black woman or man was killed by the police. I want to live long enough to have to think long and hard to remember the last time an innocent Black woman or man was lynched.

Mary E. Weems

Notes

1   See Alexander and Weems (2017).
2   See Weems (2003).

PART 1

Sounds of Blackness

∴

CHAPTER 1

Still Hanging/On: 'Strange Fruit' and 'Glory'— Songs of/as/in Protest

Or, from Stage to Page: Documenting Ideological Performance

Bryant Keith Alexander

Southern trees bear a strange fruit. Blood on the leaves and blood at the root. Black bodies swinging in the southern breeze. Strange fruit hanging from the poplar trees.

ABEL MEEROPOL (1937), BILLIE HOLIDAY (1939)

∙∙∙

One day when the glory comes. It will be ours, it will be ours. Oh, one day when the war is won. We will be sure, we will be sure.

JOHN LEGEND AND COMMON (2015)

∙∙

"'Strange Fruit' and the 'Glory' of Possibility" was performed at the International Congress on Qualitative Inquiry in 2018 as part of a panel curated by Stacey Holman Jones entitled, "Bridge over Troubled Water: Singing and Songs as Qualitative Inquiry in Troubled Times." In her invitation to participate on the panel, Stacey wrote: "Taking the ICQI theme of 'Qualitative Inquiry in Troubled Times,' I thought it would be interesting to explore what songs and singing do to help us heal and dream, to come together in sound and in silence, and to protest and push back. I'm hoping that the panel will feature, above all, your beautiful voices (indeed, a completely SUNG panel would be the dream goal, if you're up for it!)." I took the call seriously and offered a completely sung ideological performance.

Here, I offer a description of the performance with integrated logics describing how the performance was constructed as a response to the call "to come together in sound and in silence, and to protest and push back." This performative essay also serves as an example in documenting ideological performance that uses found lyrical texts—in this case, song lyrics—as primary source material within the context of building broader arguments of the power of song as protest. In other words, while this paper is its own performance, with the staged performance existing in the crafted presentation of sung and unmanipulated song lyrics without any additional narrative exposition, and without a written script independent of the lyrics, the performance was less about the pleasure of listening. Rather, it exists as an invitation into the messaging of the songs as protest, and thus, expounds on the intentionality of performance methodology as mode, evidence, and embodied process of reasoning. The paper offers an exemplar of bringing such ideological performance *from the stage to the page* as the necessary *burden of proof* in the criticality of qualitative performative scholarship.[1]

Scene 1: "Strange Fruit"[2]

(*THE PERFORMER, a Black (African-American) male enters the performance space from stage left in silence wearing a black hoodie with white lettering across the chest that reads, "I CAN'T BREATHE." The hood is pulled over THE PERFORMER's head. White earbuds sit in his ears, with the white cords streaming down his chest to connect to a cell phone that is in the front pouch of the hoodie. He appears to be listening to music, but in the moment, he is not. There is no music playing through the ear buds at this point.*)

FIGURE 1   Bryant Keith Alexander in performance

The image is at first intended to evoke Trayvon Martin, the 17-year-old Black male who was wearing a hoodie when fatally shot by George Zimmerman, a white neighborhood watch guard. On the evening of February 26, 2012 in Sanford, Florida, Martin was walking back to the house of his father's fiancée in an upscale condominium complex from a nearby convenience store. Zimmerman, a member of the community-watch saw Martin and reported him as suspicious to the Sanford Police. Moments later, a confrontation between the two individuals took place, and Zimmerman fatally shot Martin in the chest.[3] Later, *Zimmerman was acquitted.*

The hoodie's writing, "I Can't Breathe," is a reference to the Eric Garner case. On July 17, 2014, Eric Gardner, a 43-year-old African-American man died on a

Staten Island sidewalk after a police officer put him in an illegal choke hold during an arrest for selling bootleg cigarettes. The final moments of Garner's life were captured on video and publicly broadcast. His last words, "I can't breathe," became a rallying cry for the emerging Black Lives Matter protest movement. Later *a grand jury acquitted the White police officer* who choked Garner.[4] The two conflated images, hoodie and epigram, become emblematic of the current social climate and wholesale attack on Black men and boys in the United States, for which these images become signal, signifier, and symptom, as well as effigy, epitaph, and indictment in the need for protest of racial injustice. The use of the earbuds is more representative of American youth, particularly African-American youth, who carry their music with them as a connection to the rhythmicity of Black cultural life, pop culture, and maybe the lessons of resistance found in rap and hip hop.

(*THE PERFORMER centers himself relative to the audience, and in a deep baritone, he begins to sing a cappella the iconic song, "Strange Fruit." THE PERFORMER sings the song with a direct gaze sweeping the far corners and seats of the audience, inviting the mostly white audience into both the performative moment and the historical moment the song narrates in the context of the panel.*)

FIGURE 2   Meeropol, "Analysis of Strange Fruit" image

(*The song is performed at a quick clip, moving through all three verses with precision to allow the specificity of the lyrics to be punctuated by the melancholic, haunting melody. This both invokes and evokes the pained juxtaposition of Black bodies hanging from trees like fruit.[5]*)

"Strange Fruit" was first written as a protest poem by Abel Meeropol in 1937. Two years later, Billie Holiday made it one of the first songs protesting racism to be recorded in popular music. The song has continued relevance in the Trump era in response to the questions, "Do Black Lives Matter?" and "Do raced and gendered bodies, Mexicans, members of the LGBTQ+ community, and women matter with the rise of the #MeToo Movement?"[6] The song uses both metaphor and analogy to depict dead Black bodies hanging from poplar trees in the south as a strange fruit "for the birds to pluck," and "the wind to suck." The comparisons are implicitly and explicitly descriptive, for they make real the act of hanging Blacks as a public performance of pleasure, privilege and the propriety of whiteness in the South. All of which makes racism not merely "a prejudice against someone because of their race," but "a prejudice against someone because of their race, when those views are reinforced by systems of power": publicly, sometimes collectively and communally, and without sanction. [7] The incident in Charlottesville, Virginia, on August 12, 2017, in which hundreds of white nationalists, alt-righters, and neo-Nazis participated in a "Unite the Right" rally, resulting in the deaths of three counter-protesters and two police officers, is yet another testament to the ongoing struggle and consequences of and against systems of white power in/as racism.[8]

FIGURE 3   Lynching of Thomas and Abram Smith, August 7, 1930. (Source: Getty Images)

In the song, there is a juxtaposition of Black bodies *to/as* fruit, or "strange fruit," and *in/as* a "crop" to be "plucked" and "sucked." The juxtaposition of the "smell of magnolias" against "the smell of burning flesh"—a reference to other spectacular atrocities committed against Black bodies—evidences the facile disregard to whether Black lives matter, both *there and then* and in the *here and now*. This stands in relation to rampant police brutality, the dangers of driving and walking while Black in America, and the general disregard for Black civil liberties. All of which makes the song "Strange Fruit" a pained anthem to Black suffering that is pertinent not just for historical archival purposes but as a current-day protest song.

Scene 2: Glory

(*At the end of singing "Strange Fruit,"* THE PERFORMER *fumbles in the pouch of the hoodie in a disturbed and frustrated manner. He pulls out his iPhone* [*music device*] *and attempts to switch to a song in his music library. This serves as a switch from the song in his head* [*from his historical memory of "Strange Fruit," which is not really playing on the music device*] *to a song that actually emanates from the device. He makes the selection. In that moment, from a small wireless speaker that he draws from his pocket, the song, "Glory" by John Legend and Common is heard loudly broadcasting into the space. With a renewed energy,* THE PERFORMER *sings along with the chorus while staring at the audience.*)

FIGURE 4   Protesters at March on Washington. (Source: Getty Images)

"Glory," a modern-day protest song, is the lead single on the soundtrack from the 2015 movie, *Selma*.[9] John Legend and Common, who co-performed "Glory," won the category of "Best Original Song" at the 2015 Golden Globe Awards and received the Oscar for "Best Original Song" at the 87th Academy Awards. Inspired by the Civil Rights Movement and the 1965 marches from Selma to Montgomery, the song juxtaposes the unrest in Ferguson, Missouri, which was happening when the film was made, with and in relation to the history the movie narrates. The Ferguson unrest involved protests and riots beginning the day after Michael Brown, an 18-year-old Black man, was fatally shot by a white police officer named Darren Wilson, age 28, on August 9, 2014, while walking with a friend in the center of a two-way road.

The officer stated that an altercation ensued when Brown attacked Wilson in his police vehicle. As they struggled for control of the officer's gun, the weapon fired, he said. Brown and his friend, Dorian Johnson, then fled, with the officer pursuing them. Wilson stated that Brown then stopped and physically charged him after a short pursuit. In the altercation, the officer fired a total of 12 times, including twice during the struggle in the patrol car. The last bullet was the fatal shot. Brown was hit a total of six times from the front. His friend, Johnson, disputed Wilson's description of the event. Johnson said the officer had started the fight at the patrol car, and that Brown had put his hands in the air in surrender and said, "Don't shoot," after running from the vehicle.

Rampant protests, rioting and looting immediately broke out on the streets of St. Louis, and a city curfew was put in place. A grand jury was called to examine the evidence. The unrest sparked vigorous debates across the country about the relationship between law enforcement officers and African Americans, and invoked the historic legacy of sanctioned white violence against Black bodies.[10] After the murder, "Hands up, don't shoot," became the movement's slogan, with the gesture of hands up as protests against police violence.[11] In November, *the white police officer was acquitted* by the grand jury. A similar rallying cry emerged in the June 23, 2018, case of a white Minneapolis police officer who shot an unarmed Black man, Thurman Blevins. Before the white officer began shooting, Thurman was captured on body camera footage yelling: "Please don't shoot me!" "Leave me alone!"[12] *The White police officer was acquitted.*

The difference between the singing of "Strange Fruit" a cappella and the broadcasting of "Glory" from the soundtrack symbolizes the internal and external state of THE PERFORMER, representing the private versus public experiences of African Americans in general. "Strange Fruit" is used to represent a historical trauma and current daily reality that plays out in the heads, hearts and bodies of Black folks. It recognizes incidents such as the 2007 Jena Six in my home state of Louisiana, during which a group of Black teenagers beat up a white classmate after a series of escalating racial abuse. Initially the students were charged as adults suspected of attempted second-degree murder, instead of minors accused of battery. The preceding incidents included a hangman's noose being strung up in the city's trees. Its presence ultimately evoked the historical remembrance of white retaliation to the presumption of Black threat and resistance, as well as a current reality in which Black boys are still unduly "strung-up" and issued overly harsh sentences for attacking a white agitator.[13]

Presenting the song, "Strange Fruit" in this manner represents an internal monologue, a psychological trauma in the Black experience in America—hence the choice to have the audience only hear THE PERFORMER singing a cappella. And while THE PERFORMER has the earbuds in his ears, the music is not emanating from the musical device; it emanates from his soul and from history, which has a soundtrack of its own that most African-American folks can recognize. When the wireless speaker is activated for "Glory," it serves to bring the audience into the collective experience of Black folks—as commemoration, as complicity, as culpability, and/or as a call for accompaniment in the Civil Rights Movement. The song as anthem is presented in the form of a broadcast for all to hear as a public service announcement.

(On the first verse of Glory, which invokes a protest march, THE PERFORMER raises his right arm with a clenched fist. The raised, clenched fist, with thumb crossing bent fingers, is facing the audience. It appears as the iconic Black Power symbol.)

FIGURE 5   George Floyd Protest on Donald Trump's Birthday – New York (left) (Source: Getty
Images) and Bryant Keith Alexander in performance (right)

Hands to the Heavens, no man, no weapon
Formed against, yes glory is destined
Everyday women and men become legends
Sins that go against our skin become blessings.

(*In his clenched fist, THE PERFORMER clutches the mini wireless speaker to further broadcast the sound and as anthem to the message. THE PERFORMER then moves forward and marches up the aisles of the audience, while mouthing the words to the song. The first verse continues.*)

The movement is a rhythm to us.
Freedom is like religion to us,
Justice is juxtapositioning us,
Just for all just ain't specific enough.
One son died, his spirit is revisitin' us

Truant livin' livin' in us, resistance is us
That's why Rosa sat on the bus
That's why we walk through Ferguson with our hands up
When it go down we woman and man up
They say, "Stay down," and we stand up
Shots, we on the ground, the camera panned up
King pointed to the mountain top and we ran up.

(*THE PERFORMER's movement becomes more rhythmic, and he appears to be dancing as he turns and returns to center stage. THE PERFORMER arrives back to center stage in time to begin singing more fully with the chorus. Then, without looking at the wireless speaker, THE PERFORMER uses the thumb of his right finger to gradually decrease the volume. He then lowers his arm and returns the wireless speaker back into the pouch of the hoodie.*)

This transitional moment, between the notion of marching and dancing, is itself a juxtaposition of the lyrics and rhythms of the song, as well as the imagery of historical defiance and celebration that the lyrics narrate. Each is linked in the collective activity of the Civil Rights Movement and resides at the core of the African-American experience beginning with slavery as forms of remembrance, resistance, persistence, faith, and political activism—and as an essence within Black expressive culture. In deconstructed terms, these are:

- *Civil Rights*, as in the rights of citizens to political and social equality.
- *Movement*, as in a struggle for freedom and liberation, an act of changing physical location or position, or of having this changed; as in a group of

people working together to advance their shared political, social, or artistic ideas.
- *Civil Rights Movement*—also known as the African-American Civil Rights Movement, the American Civil Rights Movement and other terms—is a decades-long movement with the goal of securing legal rights for African Americans that other Americans already held or have.

Each activity is intentionally choreographed to enact collective action for a specified purpose: ceremonial public display, synergized communal outrage for a cause, collective force in defense and defiance to a happening—all with a directionality of destination and desired outcome. Political activist marches and strikes are forms of *utopian performance* "that provide a place where people come together, embodied and passionate, to share experiences of meaning making and imagination" that demand and project the possibilities "of a better world."[14] They do not just represent aestheticized performance, but are strategic deployments of performance in sociopolitical terms: *performance as contestation* with *directions of effectivity* that are both ideological and resistant, seeking to contest systems of power and literally place bodies on the line for that purpose. [15]In the last verse of the song, Common raps:

> We sing, our music is the cuts that we bleed through
> Somewhere in the dream we had an epiphany
> Now we right the wrongs in history
> No one can win the war individually
> It takes the wisdom of the elders and young people's energy
> Welcome to the story we call victory
> The comin' of the Lord, my eyes have seen the glory.

In the verse he furthers the argument of protest music as an outcry of Black pain and suffering. He invokes the elders, as in his previous reverence of Rosa Parks' performance of resistance as activism, and in Martin Luther King Jr.'s "I Have a Dream" speech calling for collective and communal activism to achieve victory. He also invokes the resonance of the King speech in relation to the "Battle Hymn of the Republic," according to which all men and women—and those in between—should stand equal and have the potential to see the glory.

The song stands as both freedom anthem and *propaganda song*, as categories of persuasion that are magnetic and rhetorical, with a motivational and invitational zeal.[16] Such songs, as described by Martin Luther King, Jr., "Invigorate the movement in a most significant way [...] these freedom songs serve to give unity to a movement, and there have been those moments when disunity could have occurred if it had not been for the unifying force of freedom songs and the great spirituals."[17] The song "Glory" in *Selma* serves that purpose within the film for the current viewing public in the context of a historical legacy. It also seeks to not only memorialize, but to reactivate participation in the Civil Rights Movement as it relates to current happenings—which are always and already the same. This building of coalitions of resistance with community as the locus of political action as site, object, and method in which ideological performance take foot as political intervention and activism.[18]

Scene 3: Reprise—"Strange Fruit Hanging"

(*After lowering his arm and returning the wireless speaker back to the hoodie pouch,* THE PERFORMER *becomes solemn with a slightly dead expression on his face.* THE PERFORMER *raises his right arm into the air. The gesture no longer appears as the iconic raised Black Power symbol. This time, the raised arm has a bent tension in it. The fist appears in a slightly inverted angle downward. It appears more like an extended grip holding something up.* THE PERFORMER *then tilts his head to the left, leaning towards his left shoulder. The imagery of extended arm, clutched fist, and tilted head simulates a lynching. The first image in performance is suggestive but made real in the minds of the audience as the second image. The image is held for about five seconds.*)

FIGURE 6   Bryant Keith Alexander in performance. "I Can't Breathe"

(*Holding the position,* THE PERFORMER *begins to sing the last verse of "Strange Fruit." But unlike the previous time, the verse is sung in a slow and methodical manner.*)

Here is a fruit for the crows to pluck.
For the rain to gather, for the wind to suck.
For the sun to rot,

for the trees to drop.
Here is a strange and bitter crop.

(*THE PERFORMER punctuates the assonance at the end of the phrasing.*)

"Plu*ck*"!
"Su*ck*"!
"Ro*t*"　　!
"Dro*p*"　　!
"Crooooooooooooooooooop"　　! <<<<<<<<<<<<<<<

(*At the end of the song, THE PERFORMER extends the word "crop" with increasing volume so that it sounds like a wail. After extending the note, THE PERFORMER slowly lowers his arm, slowly lifts and centers his head facing the audience, and then immediately exits stage left and returns to his seat.*)

FIGURE 7　　Bryant Keith Alexander in performance (Source: Jon Rou, Assistant Director, Photo and Video, Loyola Marymount University)

While evident throughout the performance in the choice of songs, delivery, staging, and purposefulness of embodied performance, the last scene makes more palpable the notion of this event as an ideological performance: a performance that seeks to foreground not only the substantive content of what is said, but the social, cultural, and political context in which it is spoken. This echoes in the words and worlds created in the text, and how they reflect the everyday world in which we live, while also emphasizing the experiencing moment of the performance and beyond. An ideological performance is a structured and embodied act that speaks not only to a system of beliefs or interpretive frames of knowing, but to a contentious positionality of being that implicates both performer and audience in a tensive struggle. The ideological performance "is the way one 'codes' one's ideology into behavior and aesthetics [consciously and unconsciously] in a way that can then be read and interpreted by others based on knowledge of the referenced meaning systems."[19]

For me, ideological performances ask and demand the audience not to reside in the comforts of entertainment. They disrupt those comforts with the challenges of thinking and feeling through complex issues of culture and community, with which they are complicit. Here, the staged, conspicuous ideological performance asks the audience to allow my presumedly privileged, educated, academic, administrative, Black/male/body to serve as a proxy for all Black (male) bodies: Trayvon Martin, Eric Garner, Michael Brown, Thurman Blevins, the Jena Six, and all the unnamed brothers and sisters lost to slavery, police, violence and racism. And thus, to realize also that I am not immune to the realities that befall those with both the materiality and historicity of African-American Blackness. I deal with the same ideological presumptions of my person every day in the places that I play, work and live. The chances of such encroachment on my person therefore not without possibility for it happens in the macro- and microaggressions of daily living, and in the implicit biases that very quickly become explicit in varying forms of social sanction. "'Strange Fruit' and 'Glory'" (the performance) is an embodied exemplification of performance as making, not faking.[20] This ideological performance illuminates and continues to work to make known the cultural experience(s) of African Americans.

The ideological performance as mode and methodology is always centered in and on the so-called "ideological body," which references all the social factors that might influence physical modes of experience and expressions of being, and of being seen in one's daily mobility in the world and in situated places of cultural encounter. It also describes the ideological body that most often precedes the physical body in the social imaginary of others, whether it exists as privileged or pained—and hence as in the lynching of Black bodies and in the white bodies who witness the lynching with pleasure. The ideological body is the (pre)anticipated and socially constructed cultural body, the race/gendered/disabled body. In other words, it's the intersectionally complex body— which of course is all of our bodies. It is the imagined body that precedes and preps the stage for social encounter. In that case, the ideological body is both particular and plural; its interpretive significance both emanates and animates from, with, and upon other bodies. It is the actual "site [or moment] of cultural inscription" that ultimately influences what that body does and knows how to do (fight or flight).[21] It determines what that body is perceived to be and to be about, whether it's pernicious and suspicious. Each ideological body—that which is naming and being named—is historically situated in fact and fiction shaping the realities of being and becoming. My Black male body is on the line in this performance and in the reporting of the performance. And "the line" itself, as much as it can be, is also an ideological construct with powerful meaning and metaphor. But for this body in public spaces, "the line" is always a fixed positionality of both risk and possibility. It is a practiced place—one of social encounter.[22]

This ideological performance used embodied strategies—hoodie, epigram, headphone, singing, music, gesture, gaze, and pose—to suggest and juxtapose the complex issues of these particular songs of protest and resistance, relative to the broader theme of the panel. This article sought to outline the scripting and staging of this conspicuous performance to illuminate the ideological arguments that are created in the juxtaposition of songs and embodied method of performance. It allows me, as actor and agent of the message, and as subject and center of the arguments, to talk about the performance "in terms of the enactment of meaning and identity within meaning systems, rather than in terms of success or failure."[23] It also suggests that the success or failure of ideological performances in everyday life, unlike the problematic and presumptive consequence in what is reductively thought of as aesthetic performance, has dire consequences on real bodies.

For you see, racism is an ideological performance: an embodied enactment of prejudice as meaning, belief, and action in a system of power with relational effects. And the historical attack on Black bodies as a performed act of racism is really a *life or death* matter. It goes beyond ideology as "a symbolic perspective regarding desired social conditions."[24] Instead, racism is an ideological performance that acts upon making a desired social condition real, sometimes with mortal consequences. Such performances also demand counter-performances of resistance as acts of survival and social consciousness. The imagery invoked in the title and actions of this ideological performance, using the iconic lyrics of both "Strange Fruit" and "Glory," conveys the fact that Blacks in these United States are *still hanging* in the literal lynching and litigation of our bodies, and in the metaphorical lynching and lambasting of our social construction. Meanwhile, our perpetual survival instinct, emboldened by a faith of transcendence and a push for activism, demands that we continue *to hang on* to the hopeful possibility of a new day.

And John Legend (and Common) sang:

> When the war is won, when it's all said and done
> We'll cry glory
> (Glory, glory) Oh (Glory, glory).

(*BLACKOUT*)

Notes

1 See Hopkins (1981) and Johnson (2012).

2 For statistics about the ever-increasing list of unarmed Black persons who have died from police brutality, see *Mapping police violence* (https://mappingpoliceviolence.org/) and O'Kane (2020).

3 See Shooting of Trayvon Martin (n.d.).

4 See Taibbi (2017).

5 The image comes from the essay: *Analysis of Strange Fruit written by Abel Meeropol.* Masters of Poems. https://mastersofpoems.weebly.com/analysis-of-strange-fruit.html (image available at: http://lencrenoir.com/wp-content/uploads/2010/06/strangefruit.jpg).

6 I am reminded that my colleague E. Patrick Johnson traveled with a performance piece entitled "Strange Fruit" that centered around issues of race, gender, sexuality, and Black masculinity. Patrick and I performed together at a couple of different venues; my own performance was entitled "Brother Scars." To be revisiting the construct of "strange fruit" nearly 20 years later is humbling—not in the construct itself, but in the fact that not much has changed in the broader social and cultural orientation of the issues to which the construct refers. E. Patrick Johnson (2003) chronicled his experiences performing "Strange Fruit" in the essay "Strange Fruit: A performance about identity politics."

Between 1998 and 2000, I traveled performing a one-man show titled, "Putting Your Body on the Line." The show, which originated as a part of my doctoral capstone project in Performance Studies at Southern Illinois University-Carbondale, explored representations of Black masculinity. That performance inspired aspects of my book *Performing black masculinity: Race, culture, and queer identity* (Alexander, 2006).

7 See Oluo (2018, p. 26).

8 See Reeve (2017, August 14): "On August 12, 2017, hundreds of white nationalists, alt-righters, and neo-Nazis traveled to Charlottesville, Virginia, to participate in the "Unite the Right" rally. By Saturday evening, three people were dead—one protester, and two police officers—and many more injured."

9 See *Glory*, Genius lyrics (https://genius.com/Common-glory-lyrics).

10 See Ferguson unrest (n.d.).

11 See Hands u, don't shoot (n.d.).

12 See Berman and Farzan (2018).

13 See The Case of the Jena Six (n.d.).

14 See Dolan (2008, p. 2).

15 See Fuoss (1997, p. 83).

16 See Denisoff (1968).

17 See Denisoff (1968, p. 243).

18 See Filewod (2001, p. 89).

19 See Fuist (2014, p. 430).

20 See Turner (1982, p. 93).

21 See Pineau (2002, pp. 43–46).

22 See Certeau (1984).

23 See Fuist (2014, p. 432).

24 See Platt and Williams (2002, p. 336).

On *Blackouts* and *Black Notes*

Bryant Keith Alexander

Dear Mary,

I am standing in a *blackout* at the end of this previous performance. I am standing in the space of darkness that is both my body and the theatrical tradition that signal the end of a performance. But also, I am standing in a type of socio-historical moment of riots throughout the country at the time of this writing; a time when the Black Lives Matter Movement has Black people out on the streets demanding a change. I am standing in a blackout waiting for the lights to come back on for the ceremonial stage bow, and for this country to get right with Black people.

Trust me, I also have a feeling of just wanting to walk away—and leave the last word of the performance as "BlackOUT," as in, "This Black man is out of here," and leave the audience to speculate in the darkness. But of course, I won't do that. In the blackout, the soulful sounds of "Glory" is still playing. It is a song that, like so many in the historical songbook of Black folks, crosses genres and traditions of Negro Spirituals, Gospel, Jazz, R&B, Rap, and Hip Hop. Songs that ring out as *black notes*: messages, signals, transcriptions, inscriptions, prayers, celebrations of survival, and anthems of hope. So, I will wait for the lights to come up to take my bow—but wanting the audience to understand the power of performance not just to entertain, but the critical work of performance in the "crisscrossing lines of activity and analysis"; performance as a work of *imagination*, as an *object of study*; performance as a *pragmatics of inquiry*, both as a model and method; performance as an *optic and operation of research*; and performance as *tactics of intervention*, creating *alternative spaces of struggle*.[1] That is what I am also learning from your work.

Oh, I see that you are next on the stage. *The curtain is opening.* I am with you, Sista. Break a leg!

Bryant

Notes

1 See Conquergood (2002, p. 152).

© BRYANT KEITH ALEXANDER, 2021 | DOI: 10.1163/9789004464858_003

Black Notes

Mary E. Weems

Original Negro Spirituals were composed of only the Black keys on a piano. Some say it was to echo the sounds coming from the bowels of slave ships. Like the Sankofa bird, which in the Akan language of Ghana means "to reach back and get it," "Black Notes" begins by returning to the past, then moving forward through contemporary moments both lived and imagined. In this performance piece, I use auto/ethnography and poetic and narrative inquiry as my methods to investigate the Black experience through a cultural lens that shifts from the personal to the political.

(*Setting: Stage is set with a short stool. Actor enters singing "Motherless Chile" and crosses stage like a weary traveler carrying a "too" heavy suitcase. She sets the suitcase down, sits on its edge, and begins.*)

Note from the Slave ship "Jesus"

We refused to go back—
they opened the hole
food and salt
burned tongues
dead flesh rotted

Noise from their mouths
Loud, foreign as skin—whips
as punctuation

No history repeated
no one to tell our stories
iron arms and legs
clear rhythm between us
Jesus pulls us further away

© MARY E. WEEMS, 2021 | DOI: 10.1163/9789004464858_004

We refused to let go of each other
our chains linked—a joke for the white men

When it was our turn, we stumbled to the deck
with many from different tribes
and when they let the locks loose
we ran from the edge, jumped
into the Atlantic laughing
out loud for our captors
who knew in that moment
they'd lost everything.

(*Kicks backwards to knock suitcase down, opens it out flat, takes out the mud cloth with reverence, covers her body with it, embraces it, then carefully spreads it out on the floor. Once it's smoothed out, she stands and sings one stanza of "Amazing Grace."*)

(*Pulls clothesline shaped like lynch rope out of the suitcase, moves to the left of the suitcase while holding up the "noose" and shaking it lightly.*)

Haiku

People used to applaud
at lynchings. Dead
bodies snapping like fingers.

(*Begins walking upstage, crosses over to mudcloth, begins snapping her fingers, getting in the mood to dance. She begins dancing, doing the "Bump" while singing "one" line from "Give up the Funk."*)

'ow we want the funk, gotta have the funk ow.'

Funk 2

I dream in funk
wants to keep the locs in my hair
suck rib bones till they pop
watch sistas braid hair in beauty shops on Saturday afternoons

stand around in my yard sayin' mothafuck this and mothafuck that
laughin' at shit that's funny just because you jivin'
find somebody who remembers the song 'Make it Funky'
line dancin' with my husband till my feet sweat
and I smell like rot gut wine
forget about everything else
'cept how good it is
to be
Black!

(*Removes xcp: Cultural Poetics Journal from suitcase. She walks slowly over to stool, sits down "properly," and reads definition.*)

Colorblind: On the Black-Hand Side. (n)[1]

Origin: (White folks). 1. An individual who has 20/20 vision 24/7 until suddenly confronted with race-hatred, a subject they're unwilling to deal with, preferring to pretend it's better to be blind in one eye and unable to see out the other; to practice saying "I do not see color" while wearing a blindfold so teeth do not fall like boulders out of both sides of their mouth. The word said when asked how many Black people they work with, teach, pass on the street, invite home, know the first names of, attend church with, while they're biting tongues to keep from saying THE EXACT NUMBER. 2. Anti-Social echo-nomic, mis-education, just-us, po-litical institutions pretending they want an equitable playing field, while promoting an a-z racist agenda. 3. (v) When someone tries so hard not to say nigger they begin fucking up the American English their ancestors created to confuse everybody: I colorblind you. We're colorblinding our home for Christmas. She colorblinded her kids before she sent them to school. 4. (adv) A euphemism added to make inhumane acts okay in the eyes of the majority of nice-white-racists who hate the Klan, but send small, annual donations so they can sleep easy at night: The police colorblind killed him. We colorblind coded the construction contracts. The counselor colorblind filed her students' college applications.

(*Drops dictionary with a thud on Mudcloth in disgust.*)

Colorblind?

(*Moves back to front of stool.*)

School on Cleveland Street

I'm in from out of town
bag full of ideas, activities, projects
designed to inspire elementary teachers
who've been in the classroom for decades.

On the ride over, I notice a mirror of my old neighborhood,
unkempt vacant lots, closed storefronts with "open" signs in the windows,
house after house living on the edge like an endless, brutally cold winter night.

(Removes child's sneaker from suitcase, sits on stool [sees child], ties shoe as if
tying it for a child, then puts it between her legs and stands back up.)

My friend turns down the street where the school is located
and I notice it's named after my hometown. I notice the nicest
building on the street is the church.

The assistant principal rushes out to greet me as the woman-guard
tells a child to get to class, speaks to us in the same sentence
and jogs off to put out the next fire on the second floor,
some small thing interrupting the flow as children pass in pulsating,
single lines guided by teachers telling them to stay quiet.

Walking the halls, watching Hope write on the walls
I'm taken back to the 1960s when all Black schools
in my neighborhood lacked air conditioning, new books,
teachers with the kind of training white teachers received.

Heart skipping a beat, like a child skipping school,
I hold back tears, make myself smile.

(Pulls large plastic ziplock bag with "D.O.A." written on the front, puts child's
sneaker in it, seals it, holds it up and in front.)

40 years disappearing as if I walked through a time warp.
Brown vs. Board echoes in my ears as I bite my tongue,
remember Obama is president,
wonder when he's been in a school like this.

(*Crosses and places bag with sneaker on Mudcloth.*)
(*Pulls ugly, bald-headed white doll from suitcase. Holds it by one-arm upside down.*)

Black Girl, White Doll

I'm in the Greyhound station
in Indiana, notice how
it looks like the world.
Different cultures waiting for a ride,
languages lilting from mouths making
air a kaleidoscope.

Standing in the sort line of new passengers
on an en route bus, children's laughter
punctuated by one mother's shout,
makes my head turn just in time to see
one dark brown face skip inside,
bald headed white baby doll clutched
to her chest like the most precious gift.

(*Drops white doll on its head on Mudcloth. Walks straight across stage, stops in front of stool. Stands.*)

Mammy

Mammy's missing from my dictionary. It leaps from mammoth to man, the in-between
a blank space for a word etched into history. Nuanced now, consumed
with our Aunt Jemima pancakes and Uncle Ben's rice.
Tyler Perry brought her back lighter, greyer, the moral messages he adds
interrupted by Gone with the Wind, Imitation of Life, Pine Sol Commercial,
and Popeye's Chicken—Honey.

(*Walks to opposite side downstage. Raises right hand, mimes putting left hand on Bible.*)

Next up in the Trayvon Martin case "Rachel Jeantel"

(Begins walking like Rachel Jeantel and circles back to sit on stool. Crosses legs, places arms across lap. Recites in "defiant" tone.)

What I Really Wanted to Say Was

Listen bald-headed, white man
you heard me the first time I rode
up and down your questions
like a sista in a low rider,
just as sure of the answers as I was
the last three times you asked me as if I
don't understand what ya'll call English.
I wanted to tell you that if I was a white girl
your ass would be winkin' and blinkin' tryin'
to see how close you could get to lookin' down
my blouse or up my skirt, that you wouldn't
be askin' me about bein' able to read cursive,
cause you'd know damn well I went to a school
that still teaches kids how to do it, also
by the way, you wouldn't give a shit about that
already knowin' the moment you looked at my white face
that I was smart, and qualified to answer all questions
one time, truthfully.
I wanted to tell you how many times nobody has come
to where most Black people live to report on those of us
who are trying our best to do the best we can in this racist,
sexist, homophobic ass country that's got the nerve to call itself the land
of the free, while steppin' on the necks of everybody Black
they can, I wanted to tell you that my dark skin
means I'm a lot closer to Africa, the Motherland than you'll
ever be, that by the time
Europe figured out how to tie its shoes
Africa had been making them for centuries.
I wanted to ask him "Why don't you ask Mr. Zimmerman
why he got out of his truck after the police officer on the other
end of his phone told him to stay in his vehicle?"
And how was it possible for Trayvon to chase
him out of his truck and begin whoopin' his ass?

And also—why in the hell Trayvon would do it
when all he was trying to do was get home.

(*Struts off stool.*)
(*Pulls high-heeled shoe from suitcase and tries to put it on, making it obvious shoe "does not fit." Drops shoe on Mudcloth. Posture changes. Walks to upstage center.*)

Barefoot

Justice: I've spent most of my life wearing high heels on the outside Timber-
lands on the inside holding up my heart like walls in an empty room. After a
girl I liked in fifth grade told me I walked like a boy, I spent weeks watching her
walk, taught myself to shift my hips from side-to-side, always feeling like a boy
on crutches, afraid any minute I'd fall and my boots would hit the ground outta
nowhere like magic. I've lived and worked in hetero world all my life, an actor
on a stage that doesn't change, Time a miserable stranger, whispers nothin' in
my ear except "maybe" and "next year." Yesterday I went to work barefoot, lived
longer than my mother who waited for a marriage, a grandchild, even a boyfriend till the day she died, her disappointment easier to bear than a truth I've
held my breath too long not to say.

(*Pulls handbag from suitcase. Clutches it to chest. Acts as if she's trying to escape
a beating/afraid. Then ceremoniously walks to and sits gingerly on stool.*)

My husband's trying to kill me

He's been practicing for 35 years. He likes my tears with his breakfast. My black
eyes fixed on his each morning after, his apology good advice on how not to get
my ass whooped next time. When company comes, he is the smile on our wedding pictures, me 15 and too dumb to know where my pee came from, mother
so happy I got a husband, she made a dress for a princess. After we were married, he kept me like a pet, a short-haired Rapunzel, unable to do anything
without permission, 10th grade education, money locked in a safe in our room.

(*Stands up.*)

He's a drunk. (*Beat*) Been one for years, brags about never stumbling or falling
in the streets, but no one sees him when he's at home tripping over me, the tip

of his gun rattling over my teeth. One time he took me out of town, the stewardess on the plane noticed the look on my face, thought I was nervous about flying, didn't know I was praying to die, that I'd taken out flight insurance and left it in my daughter's name. She gave me these little bottles of gin while he was in the bathroom.

(*Goes downstage center. Removes three small liquor bottles, holds one up, puts it back in purse. Repeats for each bottle.*)

By the time he got back, I'd drunk each one, put the empties in my purse. Held it close to my chest the rest of the flight, dumped the bottles in the airport restroom. NOW HE LIKES TO GET ME OUT IN PUBLIC AND TELL EVERYBODY WHAT A STINKING DRUNK BITCH I AM, HOW I EMBARRASS HIM, HOW HE COULD HAVE MARRIED SOMEBODY.

(*Sits back down.*)

He never looks at me anymore, never comes home except to change clothes, count his money, remind me of my place and what will happen if I ever step out if it.

(*Walks around stool. Crosses to Mudcloth. Carefully places purse down on Mudcloth.*)
(*Walks, beginning to get agitated, looks up in air, pissed off, pulls TO DO list out of pocket. Takes a seat on stool. Agitation increases with each item.*)

Deflect

[To] bend or turn aside from course or purpose. –Oxford English Dictionary

To Do:

Open mortgage mail, read for one hour.
Count to ten over and over.
Wear his boxers, give shirts to Goodwill.
Start flood in kitchen
Remove shit from ceiling fan.
Put toilet on bathroom wall.

Shave head. Buy wig.
Seal bathroom window
Fill bathtub with boiling fire.

(*Said with empathy for the man while standing with left foot resting on the stool,
as a window sill.*)

Reflect

I'm a window in a Black man's Wonderland.
Bathroom the space in the house he escapes
to when voices get too loud, bills too high,
when he wearies from wearing the world
on his head like a hard hat.

Today he enters sideways, tries to use
the toilet on the wall, opens me like a cabinet—
no fresh air. He wears fruit of the loom boxers,
a T-shirt with a hole in it, white socks
dusky from walking across floors
that haven't been washed since his wife
left, after she found out the mortgage
she thought was fixed was broke
and the house note was more than their two
salaries and a tin cup could afford.

(*Crosses stage, begins caressing breasts while circling back around stage, crosses
in front of stool, acts as if breast feeding a child while standing.*)

Beauty Secret

First thing I did when I left the doctor's office that day was take off my watch
and drop it in the trash in the pristine, all-white hallway with the carefully
polished tile floor—bright enough to see my reflection. I stood there in one
spot looking at myself until a stranger gently took my arm asked if I was okay.
Don't remember what I said to him but I knew my love affair with my beautiful
breasts was over. (*Voice change*) "We recommend double mastectomies to save
your life."

Looking back I'm still struck by the fact that I was thinking about my breasts, what time I was getting my toes done, what I'd be wearing to this year's high school reunion and...it didn't occur to me until 3 o'clock the next morning that the doctor'd told me my chances of dying from breast cancer within the next 5–10 years were 50/50 unless I had the surgery. (*Beat*)

My mother wouldn't even consider doing this to herself. Her breasts were more important to her than a chance at a longer life. Nothing, not my sister, my brother, my anger, my screaming, fear—could stop her from getting a cancer so savage it moved through her like an accidentally set forest fire. (*Beat*)

In group, women talk about tears, being afraid their significant others won't want them anymore. We laugh to keep from choking, joking about replacing our lamps with candles, breaking the mirrors, never being seen naked again. Then, in the midst of quiet conversation, one woman stops talking mid-sentence and one-by-one we all fall down, wrap our arms around each other.

There are no words for the inside job you have to do on yourself to let someone do this to you. (*Beat*)

(*Sees photographer at her feet.*)

The young photographer stoops in front of me with a clear, passionate eye and a genuine smile. He tells me I'm beautiful. Thanks me for having the courage to share this gift with others. I stand quietly in front of him naked from the waist up. Notice how like me, the two diagonal flaps that used to be my breasts look glad to be alive.

(*Removes Rose's pink sweater from suitcase, gently places it up to face and breathes. Walks like a mature man, crosses legs like a man, positions sweater carefully.*)

When a Man Loves

John: Rose has been dead 10 years and I still sleep on my side of the bed. My kids keep trying to get me to move on with my life, to get rid of the furniture we spent months shopping at secondhand stores together for, to change the way the kitchen looks, each pot and pan like a handprint, the curtains, her hair blowing in the breeze that always moved from the kitchen window and stopped the room from being hot when she was baking, to erase the 'stuff' of her as if that would make a difference. (*Beat*) I don't even remember the first time we met. It's almost as if I was on some other planet, living what I thought was a life and then one day I woke up and we were walking along Lake Erie together hand-in-hand. (*Beat*) I was explaining the shape of a cloud and what I saw and she was telling me how the water looked lit by the sun, scattered with diamonds. Why are there so many books, films, poems written about love? In the last ten years I think I've read and watched everything I could get my hands on and not one bit of it captures its essence. (*Beat*) I remember the first time I told her I loved her. We'd just made love on that old couch I used to have in my walk up apartment. I could still taste the sweet sweat of her hips, still smell what we gave each other in the air. I turned on my side to look deep into her almost-hazel eyes. They were half closed and as I leaned in to whisper in her ear, she opened her eyes and said "I already know." (*Beat*) That's how it was with us. If she wanted something special for dinner, I'd call her and suggest it. If I was troubled about the job, one of our kids, mama's health, anything, it was like she could read my mind and before I could make myself put it to words, she'd bring it up at the kitchen table, or leave a note on the dashboard of my car, or just open her arms when I got home, and ask me what was wrong. (*Beat*) She was the other side of my midnight, my baby, the exhale to my inhale, and what nothing in this world that's ever been created about love can ever prepare you for—is how to live without it.

(*Gently places Rose's sweater back in suitcase.*)
(*Removes jock strap from suitcase. Mimes putting it on, then hangs it on edge of the suitcase. Moves like a "young" jock to downstage center.*)

Locker

I quit the team
told the coach lie number four hundred and eighty-seven,
told him I was afraid of concussions, of breaking bones,
mine or someone else's, of using drugs to get better,
on-line seductive advertising making promises to jocks
nothing can keep without consequences.
I'll never forget coach's look—long and deep
kind that cuts through bullshit so fast, you can't get your walls up
to block it. He shook my hand, wished me well, told me to take
some time, to think—I almost laughed, knowing in that moment

he didn't know me any better than the rest of my teammates
my reputation hard but fair, a guy you could count on to leave practice
last, get there before anybody else, until today,

(*Sees photo in back of locker.*)

no one noticing the picture of my lover on the back wall of my locker

(*Touches lip*)

my red mouth print
on his lips.

(*Moves to suitcase, kneels down behind it then rises up, begins singing.*)

Backfire

"Don't know why, there's no sun up in the sky, Stormy weather.
We Shall Overcome, We Shall Overcome, We Shall Overcome
We Shall Overcome, Some— (*says*)day." (*Beat*) Damn, again?
What happened this time?

(*Looks up.*)
Oh yeah, took a minute, but it's coming back, Black, that's what
happened, I came back again Black, a man, in America
landed on another street, stopped by another cop,
dragged. Yeah, it's all coming back now like the f'd up ending
to a movie. What time is it?

(*Looks at watch.*)

Yep, stopped again, exact moment, 11:59 p.m.—watch keeps time by heartbeat,
by breaths,
by months, by years, by centuries. (*Beat*) This time my name's Tommy,
Just turned 21, tonight a party for a lifetime, everybody I love was there.
Mama made a cake that had so many layers she had to roll it in on a cart,
everybody singing happy birthday to me, 5th after 5th of Rose, 40s of
Beer, my girl Laura was there, daddy even brought out his stash of lightnin'

(*Beat*) I'd just whopped my brother and baby sister at a game of spades, thought I'd take the short cut home, but my car stopped on me at the red light at 79th street. (*Beat*)

Tried to start it—nothing. While I was waiting to try it again the po-lice rode up.

Cop on the driver's side rolled down his window to say something to me just as I turned my key to try it again, the light changed, pa-pow!

My ride backfired, and jerked off all in that same moment. (*Beat*) I lost time, everything moving in slow motion, the sirens, cop cars coming from every-where, and all I could think was—if I can just get home, I'll be alright, if I can just get home I'll be alright, then pa-pow!

(*Stand up*)

Window shatter, shouts, hatred, my blood, last breath, (*Beat*)

(*Sees pole.*)

Time for teddy bears and balloons on project poles, in my name, in my honor.

(*Closes suitcase.*)
(*Carries suitcase to downstage center while humming then singing "Motherless Chile." Sits on suitcase.*)

Going Home

My name's Sadie. I'm only 60 years old, but sometimes I feel like I've been here forever. Like now. When I start thinking bout Black people, bout how we're scattered like wind all over this world, my whole body hurts. It's like everything we've ever endured sets on my back like a snowy mountain.

I wanta go home. The one place in this world I should be able to lock my door and rest. (*Beat*)

Yesterday, the sheriff came to put me out of a home that's been in my family for ten generations.

Vulture who had me sign a piece-a paper to save it—that really meant he could take it—was nowhere around. And I don't have a place to put my head. (*Beat*) I'd already sold everything I could and the only thing I had left was what was in my suitcase. (*Beat*)

Last Week I Lost My Son

He didn't make it through his first day-a being 21. Bullet to the head by a po-lice officer who swore on 'his' mother and a stack-a bibles that Jimmy attacked him in his car for no reason and tried to take his gun. My son who was on his way to a full ride at Morehouse. My son who'd take time to catch flies in the house during the summer to keep from having to kill them.

I've lost so many men in my life, I have to keep a list in my dresser drawer so I can read 40 years of murder out loud. First husband. Favorite uncle. Fifteen cousins. (*Audible sigh.*)

Between the po-lice killing them fast as white folks used to lynch them, killin' each other, life dream killings and the penitentiary, Black men are in danger of becoming extinct.

Long time ago Patty Labelle sang this song made famous in a movie about home and rainbows and happy. (*Beat*)

I forgot most of it but all day long I've been singin' some-a the words and I don't even know why. "If happy little bluebirds fly, above the rainbow, why oh why can't I?"

(*Crosses to upstage center—behind Mudcloth. Bows.*)

The End

Note

1   See Weems (2006). Black Note #4 re-printed with permission from editor Mark Nowak.

Confluences of Pain

Bryant Keith Alexander

Dear Mary,

There are three lines in the upcoming pieces that haunt me. The first two lines are like those famed "two roads [that] diverged in a yellow wood" in that oft recited but empty Robert Frost poem about White people with choices. The line, "Let the People see what they did to my Child," comes into a painful confluence with, "Adult Black men crying for their mothers is more common than most people think." And here you will see that I moved from the notion of "diverged" as a thing done—like ritual choices afforded to whites and not Blacks— to a confluence: a turbulent crossing of rivers, or in this case, streams of consciousness. Not just a confluence of thought processes, but lifelines and racialized perceptions that become enactments of disregard, one on the other. A confrontation of wills made manifest in a lack of choices and predictable consequences. Our brothers Emmett Till and George Floyd, whose deaths ignited civil rights movements 65 years apart were always joined with other brothers like Rayshard Johnson. And as you also note so importantly: "White police are killing Black women too." Our sisters Sandra Bland, Breonna Taylor, and so many others—including our trans sistas/brothas, who are both particular and plural—who *sojourned their truth* came into a confluence with white authority. They were not given choices as to which path they would travel. They were forced to take the road too often traveled by Black people in this country and given no opportunity to revel in the contentment of their choice at the end, because there were no positive reflections on those outcomes. And their mothers, like Mary Mother of Jesus, only got to claim their bodies and hear the echoes of their cries through history.

Bryant

Let the People See What They Did to My Child

Mary E. Weems

(Emmett Till's mother has just returned from the funeral home to view her son's body for the first time. She is in her front room, sitting in the middle of the couch [the only set piece on stage] in a blue dress, with one of her son's Sunday hats laying beside her. Lights up.)

Mamie:

I've been crying so long, when I blink my eyes they feel full of dirt, my eye-balls so dry, even splashing them with cold water doesn't help…They dry right away, like an ice-cold wind is blowing across my face. This was one of Bobo's favorite dresses, he always said it made me look like I was wearing the sky on a summer day. When I got home, my quiet kitchen was full. Friends, family, neighbors had stopped by to leave all kinds of food. Never could figure out why, when somebody beloved dies, the first thing we do is find something to take to the house. Fried chicken, barbecue, pound cake, peach cobbler, collard greens, homemade rolls, cornbread, something, so the people grieving have one less thing to worry about. We pray, send cards with prayers and condolences, over and over as if…Walking toward the funeral home so slow I made myself count each step to keep me going in the right direction, I caught a smell in the warm breeze that made me drop to the ground, my knees scraping on the sidewalk, my head snapped back like somebody grabbed my hair. It shot up my nose so fast for a moment I couldn't breathe, all I could do was smell…my son's death the only thing in the air even though I was at least three blocks from where his body was. I'd never smelled someone dead before like that. Sure there's always been a slight odor in every funeral home I've ever been in, the smell of what happens to a body after the spirit leaves…but this was like all the Black people who have ever died in Chicago died when my son did, and even now, sitting here in my own house, it fills my nose like a putrid cement…I haven't eaten since I got the call…My brother Moses' voice choked with tears, his words coming out one at a time, leaving me to try to string them together and even when he was finished, I kept asking him: What did you say? Who are you talking about? What happened? Who's dead? I finally hung up on him without even

© MARY E. WEEMS, 2021 | DOI: 10.1163/9789004464858_006

realizing it. The idea that Bobo, my 14 year-old, one and only, boy who made me laugh first thing in the morning before I set off to work like it was his job... My son who cooked and cleaned and washed like he was a daughter, to make sure I had as little to do as possible when I came home after a long day. I kept thinking, God damn it, I didn't want him to go in the first place...Nothing good mama ever told me happens in the south to a Black man, boy, woman or child when white folks are involved...especially white women. It was the first time, Bobo had ever been, and my brother didn't even invite him, knowing how I feel about it, just told him he was going, and my Bobo kept begging me to go till I said, Yes. I gave him his daddy's ring before he left, slept with it under my pillow the night before, prayed over it, talked to God, asked him to bless it, to protect my son till he got back home...Money, Mississippi. What kind of name is that for a town? Sounds like a place slave owners' got rich buying and selling slaves, and still thought they should own us. My father and brother walked arm-in-arm with me to the casket, holding me close, waiting for me to collapse, but I yanked my arms free, told them I don't have time to be fainting now, I got work to do. I walked on my own two feet a little ahead of them, till I got to the open casket, smell of death so thick, it covered what was left of my only child, and I just stood there not wanting to see, unable to look away. All of what made him a boy was gone, his head swollen like a rotten watermelon, left in the sun, one eye hanging out like it had been pulled, the other gone...the bridge of his nose chopped up like meat run through a grinder, his pretty teeth, the ones he used to use to smile at me, broken and gone, except for two...I looked for his ears, like mine they used to curve away from his head at the ends, but I couldn't see them. All I could see was a hole where they used to be, a hole that started on one side of my baby's head and went through the other, letting in the room's light...The Bryant's didn't even leave his head in one piece, it looked like they'd taken an ax, done their best to chop it in half, before they used barbed wire to tie him to a fan, dump him in the Tallahatchie river like garbage...I stood there so long, so still, I didn't even notice daddy and my brother had taken a seat to wait. Next thing I knew, the Funeral director had walked up to put his arm around me, to ask me if I wanted him to work on Bobo, make him look more presentable for the funeral, or maybe a closed casket would be better...First time I'd raised my voice since my brother called to tell me that my son died for whistling at the white woman who sold him some bubble gum in her grocery story. I said, No! Do what? Stuff the hole in his head, put his eye back in its socket, make his face look like skin, close his mouth so you can't see the almost empty hole? No! Leave him, leave my son just like he is, so everybody can see, what they did to my child and never forget it, the longest day they live.

(*She picks up Emmett's hat, takes a moment to caress the brim, puts it on her head. Lights out.*)

The End

CHAPTER 4

George Floyd's Mama

Mary E. Weems

Mama's an African word.
When I heard George Floyd's
shout, he took me
all the way back
to how we got here.

Back to most of our first words,
how we learned to speak,
walk, hold hands, cry.

I watched Black man, blood,
brother, on his stomach,
say please, say I can't breathe
Sir

the white knee disguised as blue
on his neck, cop's hands in his
pockets as if relaxed, as if all is well,
as if that's not a man
trapped on the ground
for eight minutes and forty-six seconds.

I realized this cop would not
have done this to a dog.
His exception so natural,
it didn't occur to him to let up
when Floyd begged for air,
his polite desperation ignored
by three cops who stood around
as if watching a movie,
without the popcorn.

© MARY E. WEEMS, 2021 | DOI: 10.1163/9789004464858_007

It is broad daylight.
People are witnessing and recording,
when Floyd screams
and his dead mama comes
to pick him up,
as God releases him from his body
so she,
can take him home

Wendy's, Me, and Rayshard Brooks: Another Black Man Killed (June 12, 2020)

Bryant Keith Alexander

My birth date is June 12. On June 12, 2016, Omar Mateen, a 29-year-old "security guard" killed 49 people and wounded 53 others in a mass shooting inside the gay night club Pulse in Orlando, Florida, United States. Orlando police officers shot and killed him after a 3-hour standoff. As a gay man, I immediately began to mourn the loss of my LGBTQ+ family members under those circumstances. And I began to write. A part of that writing joined in collaboration with Mary E. Weems in what became a dedicated Special Issue with twenty (20) other scholars/artists/activists writing on the subject.[1] On June 12, 2020, I find myself commemorating another atrocity on my birthday at the intersections of my being a Black/gay/man in America. The issues of racism, sexism, homophobia, and hate are already and always interconnected for many of us.

When I was 15 years old, I worked at a Wendy's restaurant on the frontage road off the I-10 Freeway in Lafayette, Louisiana. I worked for nearly 6 months raising money for a school choral trip to Hawaii. I really was working to make sure that my mother could travel along as a chaperone. It was a personal gift to her. You see, along with my father, my mother worked tirelessly to help support her seven children. And when we wanted to "do good," as she would say, she would bend over backwards to see us advance even further. But she never thought about herself. So, while she was pinching pennies to make sure that I could make that choral trip, I got permission to take the job at Wendy's to help make it possible for her to travel along as a chaperone. It would be her first plane ride. We made the trip. That was a little over 40 year ago.

> *On June 12, 2020, Rayshard Brooks, a 27-year-old Black man, was fatally shot by police at a Wendy's drive-thru in Atlanta, Georgia, after officials said he resisted arrest [...]*

> *Protesters on Saturday [the day after the killing] set fire to the Wendy's restaurant where Brooks was killed and shut down an interstate highway in both directions. At least 36 people were arrested, police said.[2]*

© BRYANT KEITH ALEXANDER, 2021 | DOI: 10.1163/9789004464858_008

I hated working at Wendy's.

I hated everything about it: constantly having to stare at the image of the redheaded, freckled-faced, pony-tailed pixy namesake of the franchise, the apple of her father's eye, who probably didn't have to work a job as a high school student to give her hard-working mother a gift.

I hated the smell of the place and how I smelled when I was done working. The smell of cooking those square patties and those thick fries permeated my skin. And there was a smell of racism that I could not wash off.

As much as I hated the general clientele on late weekend nights, people coming from and going to the clubs through the drive-through window, the games they wanted to play to barter for food or pull away without paying—a surveillance camera captured license plates; the rule of thumb was "get the money first before you give the food"—what I hated even more were the police cars that circled the strip of fast food restaurants: Wendy's, Taco Bell across the street, a Pizza Hut, then a McDonald's. Not unlike the bar hopping clientele, the police officers also lingered. They lingered partially as security, but also because many of the restaurants supported informal discounts for police in uniform on the strip. And the police took advantage, continually strolling up to the drive-through windows for free burgers and fries, or refills on sodas and Frosties. Their arrogance offended me, and I never felt safe.

> *Police said Brooks fell asleep in the Wendy's drive-thru on Friday night and had failed a sobriety test. When police tried to take him into custody, Brooks resisted and stole a Taser from an officer, they said. Brooks ran from the officers, and at one point, aimed the Taser at police before the officer fired his weapon...*

I remember my manager, a white man in his early 40's who was making a career at Wendy's, often had his finger on fast dial to the circling police. Every time Black customers came into the store after 9 p.m., if they spoke in a tone that he didn't like, or swaggered in a way that suggested they had been drinking, or just arrived together in any group of three Black folks, he would say to the white employees, "Watch out—those niggers are coming in. Don't take no shit. I am calling the police." And I stood there, a 15-year Black boy in the signature Wendy's puffy blue and white stripped hat and shirt, dropping fries or pressing patties or dressing hamburger buns, standing as both witness to and victim of the white vehemence of that manager's authority. Each action, his and mine, were routines of daily work in Wendy's—and of living in the South.

Brooks was taken to a local hospital where he died after surgery, officials said. One officer was treated for an injury and discharged from the hospital […] It was said that Brooks had planned on taking his 8-year-old daughter skating for her birthday but never came home. "She had her birthday dress on. She was waiting for her dad to come pick her up and take her skating." […] Brooks has three daughters, ages 1, 2 and 8, and a 13-year-old stepson […] He was said to be beloved by family and friends. "We watched [his children] play and laugh and be oblivious to the fact that their dad was murdered on camera, a scene that we keep repeating."

The news coverage of the protest the day after the killing included this image that I love to hate:

The image of the Wendy's restaurant on fire during protests on Saturday June 13, 2020, where Rayshard Brooks was shot and killed by police that Friday evening.

FIGURE 8   A man walks by as the Wendy's restaurant is on fire during protests on Saturday, June 13, 2020, where Rayshard Brooks was shot and killed by police. (Source: Brynn Anderson, AP Images)

I love to hate the image of Wendy's burning because of the multiple juxtapositions. The shadowed image of the redheaded, freckled-faced, pony-tailed pixy namesake of the franchise on the building, against the equally red flames of the fire marking the scene of the crime. The marketing message, "Quality: Service That Doesn't Cut Corners," on the building against the backdrop of the murder of another Black man in America by police. And the juxtaposition in my current reality as a grown Black man in America and my childhood memory of working at the Wendy's restaurant on the frontage road off the I-10 Freeway in Lafayette, Louisiana—with a drive-through window that looked just like that one—with sluggard police officers wanting refills on their sodas and Frosties. I wonder if the manager at that Atlanta, Georgia, Wendy's restaurant called the police that murdered Rayshard Brooks. I wonder if that manager, maybe a white man in his early 40's who was making a career at Wendy's, also had his finger on fast dial to summon the circling police officers to get the suspicious nigger sleeping in his car. Was he sleeping?

He had planned on taking his 8-year-old daughter skating for her birthday but never came home. "She had her birthday dress on. She was waiting for her dad to come pick her up and take her skating."

Police said Brooks [...] ran from the officers, and at one point, aimed the Taser at police before the officer fired his weapon, the Georgia Bureau of Investigation said, citing surveillance video that was released to the public.

I imagine that whether he was sleeping or not, the panic of seeing a police officer beckoning him out of his vehicle was alarming. I imagine that the tone and tenor of the search and seizure put him into a fight-or-flight mode, a struggle against the social realities of so many of his brothers and sisters—our brothers and sisters—who have found themselves dead after such encounters. I imagine that his understandable panic fueled—but did not cause—the reality of his murder. Almost like a pained prophecy of such encounters, a pained morality play with or without a moral, but with a familiar cast of stock characters playing out a groundhog's day ritual of Black men encountering police officers, always with the same tragic ending.[3] And if, "Morality plays typically contain a protagonist who represents either humanity as a whole or a smaller social structure," while, "Supporting characters are personifications of good and evil," it is hard to figure out how *justice and equity* play out in this national drama, in these United States of America.[4]

Black men in America have no perceptions of such a situation, other than what history has documented, what the nightly news broadcasts, and what our obituaries read. So, we struggle for our manhood as we struggle for our lives: against those who have sworn to serve and protect. Our Black bodies are under surveillance alright, but not for *our* protection; they are monitored for the defense of "peace officers" out hunting freed negroes, whether wearing body cameras or depending on surveillance cameras at local white establishments.

I wonder about Rayshard Brooks' mother. Like my mother, I am sure she never thought about herself in relation to her children, always selflessly laboring for their advancement. I wonder if, like during George Floyd's 8 minutes and 46 seconds, Rayshard cried out to his mother when it was apparent that his Black Life Did Not Matter at that damn Wendy's drive-through window in Atlanta, Georgia. Adult Black men crying for their mothers is more common than most people think, because Black men are depicted as indestructible. To depict us in that way makes it easier to destroy us. But our mothers are the ones who know us and love and shelter us into being. I lost my mother in 2013 to a drunk driver. It seems that I've cried out to her every day since—and now, ever more.

Nearly 40 years ago, I left Wendy's physically safe, but not without scars. When I was sure that I had raised enough money to take my mother along on the trip as a chaperone, I quit that job at Wendy's and never looked back. I never went to a Wendy's again. The job served no other purpose for me, though as a 15-year-old boy I did become more woke to racism.

I am glad to see that *the former Atlanta police officer who shot Rayshard Brooks in the back after he resisted arrest and ran off outside a Wendy's fast-food restaurant will be charged with felony murder and aggravated assault with a deadly weapon, according to a Georgia district attorney.*

I am glad to see the recognition that *"Mr. Brooks never presented himself as a threat," said Paul Howard, the local district attorney for Fulton County.*[5]

Now we will see if justice will be denied again, as it has been in so many similar cases. I mourn for Rayshard Brooks, his children, his family, and his mother. I mourn for the countless number of Black people taken by police brutality.

Black people have no business going to Wendy's.

Notes

1 See Alexander and Weems (2017).
2 All italicized quotes throughout this essay are taken from the article Carissimo and McNamara (2020).
3 See Now This. Groundhog Day for a Black Man' Shows Danger Black Men in America Face (https://www.youtube.com/watch?v=tbTrsfvJcJA).
4 See Morality plays (n.d.).
5 See Jarve (2020).

Where's the Beef?

Mary E. Weems

For: Rayshard Brooks, 27-year-old Father of 4 Killed 6-12-20

White police are killing Black people so fast,
we don't have time to take a breath, honor our dead,
get back to what's left of normal

White police are killing Black men so fast,
We have to write their names on our memories
in indelible ink, share their stories
with as many as possible

White police are killing Black women,
white police are killing Black women too,
but few marches happen in the streets
and their stories don't repeat in news that likes to re-show
videos.

There is no video of Sandra Bland, arrested
for a traffic stop, hung on a garbage bag in jail
where you're supposed to be safe until you either make bail,
or have your day in court

White cops are killing Black women too, but when they no-knocked
into Breonna Taylor's place, catching her in bed, looking for someone
who was already in jail, the police still shot her innocence,
eight times.

Are Black men's lives worth more?
Are Black non-hetero lives worth less?

Four hundred and one years later,
we're still treated like chattel err cattle,
our value the only group being debated,

© MARY E. WEEMS, 2021 | DOI: 10.1163/9789004464858_009

immediate response to Black Lives Matter, making it clear
ours don't, but "blue" and "all" (read white) always have
and why always ask about "Black on Black crime?"

When it comes to us it's always about everything else but what it is,
blaming the victim, the standard go-to, to deflect from the problem
at hand

Why do Blacks think we're entitled to be treated according to what America
says it is, when we were brought here for our asset value,
carefully documented in ships logs their bottom line
our asses, the same ones that in 2020
can't walk, drive, jog, sleep, breathe, be, without cops
losing our lives.

It's time for the hunted to tell the story,
and thanks to cell phone videos and police body cameras,
maybe some of us will live long enough to do it

because 18 days after George Floyd's neck succumbed to a cop's knee,
after 8 minutes and 46 seconds

18 days after he repeated, *I can't Breathe* 16 times,
following no resistance and calling the cop killing him *Sir*

18 days later while global protests continued, Floyd was buried,
the world kept watching, Rayshard Brooks stopped at "Where's the Beef,"
Wendy's, his few drinks causing him to doze in the driveway, the cops called,
they wake him up, he asks to walk to his sister's, they breathalize him, he fails,
resists, is chased like patter-rollers used to do slaves,

Brooks grabs a taser, points it behind him, tries to run-a-way, and winds up shot
in the back by cop who believed for a Black man, falling asleep
waiting in line for food
is a crime.

A Moment of Prayer

Bryant Keith Alexander

Dear Mary,

I am thinking about prayer.

Prayer: A solemn request for help or expression of thanks addressed to God or an object of worship in a cosmology of belief.

See: Yearning.

I am writing on June 19th, commonly celebrated by African Americans as Juneteenth. Juneteenth—also known as Freedom Day, Jubilee Day, and Celebration-Liberation Day—is an African-American holiday celebrated to commemorate June 19, 1865, when Union Army General Gordon Granger read federal orders in Galveston, Texas, stating that all previously enslaved people in Texas were free, ending slavery in the United States two-and-a-half years after President Abraham Lincoln's Emancipation Proclamation had become official on January 1, 1863. Justice delayed indeed is justice denied—a denial that still persists even now. African Americans recognize and celebrate that day, while also recognizing the level of struggle that Black Americans continue to face to be truly equal and truly free. We celebrate Juneteenth with resistance and critique because in this country, we must still proclaim that Black Lives Matter. We celebrate Juneteenth with solemnity and prayer.

Bryant

© BRYANT KEITH ALEXANDER, 2021 | DOI: 10.1163/9789004464858_010

Three Meditations on Prayer and Particularity

Or: On Black Mothers, Social Justice, and Queering Catholicism

Bryant Keith Alexander

Goputyourselfonyourknees[1]

My mother was what many in my childhood neighborhood would call a "good Catholic girl." For her seven children raised in a small two-bedroom house in Lafayette, Louisiana, she made sure that God was present in our house and in our lives. I honor her spirit every time I go to church. I honored her in the years of serving as an altar boy, in the years of singing in church choirs, in the years of teaching catechism, in the years of serving as a lecturer, and in the years of serving as a Eucharistic minister. I honor her and the faith that she taught me.

One of the deep and important memories of my mother that has been present for me lately is that my mother was the one who taught me how to pray. Sometimes in collective family prayer, when little bodies lined up in the church pew on Sunday, and other holy days of obligation, but also when those same small and growing bodies lined up along the couch in our home. My mother made us pray the rosary. And my mother made us take turns saying "The Lord's Prayer" softly and with reverence. She would often say, "Slow down. Say it with meaning. Say it with belief and not just as another thing memorized and recited."

"Stop," she would say. "Start it again."

"Do you believe what you just said? It's not just the Lord's prayer that he gave to us. It is your prayer that you give to the Lord." And in that lesson, she would often ask us to shift the plural to the particular, from "our" to "*my* Father." It was a lesson to particularize prayer, and when shared in a community of faith, the "our" and the "us" would have a depth of collective meaning that all who profess those words shared a common faith and commitment to one God.

One of the greatest sins that we could commit as kids was being unkind to each other. Fighting, name calling, or disrespecting each other as siblings ended with two phrases. First, "When mommy and daddy are gone, all you will have is each other. So, love one another."

Second, she would say, "Goputyourselfonyourknees." A phrase delivered with such quickness, and often with such pain, that the words blended into one single utterance that pointed to a place and an action: "Go put yourself on your knees" and pray for forgiveness. And we knew what we had to do and where: a corner of the living room under the image of a crucified Jesus. She required a slow repetition of The Lord's Prayer with emphasis on the particular: "*my* father," "give *me*," "*my* daily bread," "forgive *me*, as I forgive those who trespass against *me*." "Lead *me* not into temptation" and "deliver *me* from evil." I remember those directives as both punishments and forced moments of reflection—moments of discernment using *my* prayer to the Lord as a means of contemplating *my* actions that brought *me* to that moment, and to imagine what would be the difference in *me* that would follow prayer.

Over the years, while I continued to say prayers, I believe that until recently I didn't realize that I had forgotten how to pray. I moved back into the reciting of memorized lines getting caught up in the delivery of the script, or in the collective recitation of a congregational chant. Sometimes I even felt a little frustrated with the a-syncopated rhythms of others collectively reciting The Lord's Prayer. Until recently, I had forgotten the lessons on my knees with my mother saying, "Slow down. Say it with meaning. Say it with belief and not just as another thing memorized and recited."

"Stop." she would say. "Start again."

"Do you believe what you just said? It's not just the Lord's prayer that he gave to us. It is your prayer that you give to the Lord. He is listening." And when said in a congregation of others, it becomes a chorus of faith with its own harmonies of community activity.

Recently, I took part in an 8-week season-of-Lent program entitled "Meeting Christ in Prayer" sponsored through the Loyola Marymount University Center for Ignatian Spirituality. Our small threesome gathered for weekly meditation and contemplation. We would key in on the lessons taken from the readings of the week and give voice to our feelings: different but always co-informing. These were vulnerable moments of shared reflection in which each found his or her own personal process of sense-making and own orientation to meeting Christ in prayer. During that time, I began to remember. I began to remember my mother's lessons. And I began to learn how to pray again. Our sessions always began by reading together, and in the company of each other, "A Prayer by St. Anselm of Canterbury." The prayer has touched a place in my heart and has reminded me of my mother's lessons in prayer as a direct address to the Lord. It reads:

> O my God, teach my heart where and how to seek you, where and how to find you.
>
> You are my God and you are my all and I have never seen You.
>
> You have made me and remade me,

You have bestowed on me all the good things I possess,

still I do not know you.

I have not yet done that for which I was made.

Teach me to seek you.

I cannot seek you unless you teach me

or find you unless you show yourself to me.

Let me seek you in my desire,

let me desire you in my seeking.

Let me find you by loving you,

let me love you when I find you.

Amen

And now, every day, I take my mother's directive to "Goputyourselfon-yourknees" as ritual practice. Not as a punishment but as a possibility of finding myself again in faith and prayer. My mother would be tickled because I also purchased a prayer kneeler that I have placed in the corner of my home office. There, "I put myself on my knees" voluntarily in a daily examen of my own being and becoming in Christ.

On Social Justice, Black Lives Matter and the Power of Prayer[2]

As a Black Man in America, I pray.

As a Black Man in America, I pray to transform self and society.

As a Black Man in America, I pray that God bless all vulnerable populations in the continued COVID-19 health crisis, and those most vulnerable to historical injustices.

As a Black Man in America, I mourn with the family and the country over the death of George Floyd, yet another unarmed black man who died at the hands of a police officer. There but for the grace of God go I.

As a Black Man in America, I pray that God Bless the Black Lives Matter movement for its continued critical advocacy and activism for social justice, and for it to publicly disassociate from factions that promote and further perpetuate fear, violence, and destruction linked with blackness. Such acts of terrorism muddle the critically importance of the Black Lives Matter movement: their work—our work—fighting for the civil liberties and protections guaranteed to all citizens of the United States of America, and particularly recognizing Black and Brown people as equal human beings under God and government, is critical to our survival.

As a Black Man, Dean of the College of Communication and Fine Arts at Loyola Marymount University in Los Angeles, I speak for all disciplines and faculty within my purview: Art and Art History, Communication Studies, Theatre Arts and Dance, Marital and Family Therapy, and Music. We understand the importance of activism and protest through rhetoric, debate, and critical artistic expression; the arts as a reflective, reflexive, and refracting mirror of self and society; and communication as art and art as communication promoting social understanding, advocating for social equality, and standing on the right side of justice in the acts of information, formation, and transformation forming part of our mission. These are our commitments to our students. These are our commitments to our society. We condemn all forms of racism and bias, and we must all fight collectively to address persistent inequities.

As a Black Man in America, and as Dean of the College of Communication and Fine Arts at Loyola Marymount University, the premiere Catholic/Jesuit university on the West Coast, I pray that God Bless this City of Angels—Los Angeles—and all cities around the Unites States impacted by this current socio-political moment.

As a Black Man in America, I pray that God Bless All Lives.

As a Black Man in America, I continue to pray for peace.

As a Black Man in America, I believe in the power of prayer.

My Mother Used to Tell Me[3]

On my desk in my home and work offices sits a picture of my parents. It is my favorite picture of them. They are dancing in an embrace that they pause only for the photographic moment. In the photo, my father has his signature sun-shades on to protect his always sensitive eyes. My mother looks directly into the camera lens with a full smile. I imagine that she is always looking at me, reminding me of the man she wanted me to be.

I always look at that picture of my parents—and particularly that image of my mother looking back at me—when I am on the phone or about to write that email that might shatter someone's reality. I look at my mother looking and smiling at me, and I pause. And while I still deliver the message that I need to communicate, from time to time, I might soften the tone and edge of the delivery or invite them to a meeting. I do this in the process of performing my academic and administrative role with humanity. My mother taught me about care, conviction, and character. And through the photo and my memory of her, she reminds me every day about the man she wanted me to be. In most cases, I imagine that she is proud. So, in reference to that daily ritual in the memori-alizing of my parents who are both long passed, I offer you additional glimpses into things my mother taught me throughout my childhood about the intersec-tion of my queer and Catholic identity.

• • •

My mother used to tell me that I was made in the image of God.

My mother used to tell me that she saw a light and joy in me that could give comfort and care to others, and that it was my responsibility to do so.

My mother used to tell me to be consistently present in my whole self, in my whole person—but always to give thanks to God for the many gifts and partic-ularities that he has bestowed upon me.

My mother used to tell me to honor my own spirit, and to respect my mind and body.

My mother used to tell me that, "God does not make mistakes."

• • •

So as far back as I can remember, my mother told me these things as lessons to live. She would tell me these things:

Sometimes triggered by things that I said or did, or that happened to me.

Sometimes triggered by my hurt feelings from childhood name calling: fag, sissy, punk, queer. Names that were hurled at me with the intent to hurt and shame a still-developing self-identity.

Sometimes triggered by thuggish pro-masculine-heterosexual male bullying when my interests turned to the gentle arts—fine, performing, literary, and communication arts—with an unwavering commitment to social justice, rather than playground brawls and bullying.

And sometimes she would tell me these things after church when someone in robed authority had uttered rigid religious rhetoric that attempted to delimit the importance of my being in the world. And once, in that not-often-discussed time when, as an altar boy, that same hypocritical robed authority lured me into an inappropriate act that challenged my belief in God. I told my mother, and she quickly reinforced to me that adults taking sexual advantage of children is abuse, not love, and that the robed authority was acting on the desire of man, not God. She then she walked over to the church to confront and report the culprit.

For you see, my mother knew of my gay identity before the happening. And in some ways my mother knew of my gay identity long before I could fully articulate it on my own terms (Psalm 139). She loved me fully and sheltered me consistently. My mother's faith in God and the Church was not challenged, but her faith in those who did not practice what they preached was shaken.

• • •

I am the fourth boy of five boys, and I had another brother who was also gay. And it would take years before my older brother Nathaniel and I would talk about what we shared. The occasion of such discussion came only after he used one of the private mantras from my mother to comfort me. I repeated others to him. And we would laugh. We laughed thinking that we were alone in our struggle but always in the comfort of our mother. And through that laughter, we recognized what our mother had been doing all of our lives: comforting, caring, and encouraging her two boys—who happen to be gay—to be fully present in their faith and in their particularity, and encouraging us to find a mindful and respectful balance in each.

My brother and I came to understand that my mother was offering lessons for being in God's presence as we were reared in a Catholic household. She offered a series of lessons that supported our particularity without demonizing our character, spirit, and potentialities. She encouraged use to live fully alive, as whole persons present. But we understood that her encouragement was not a blessing on our sexuality. It was a Catholic mother's love for her children that was relentlessly supportive of each of us as children of God.

• • •

My mother was what many in my childhood would call a "good Catholic girl," and still what others would call a "God-fearing woman." But she would always resist the Old Testament notion of a wrathful God that we should fear, because as she would say, "If your hearts are good, then God knows it." There was no need to fear him.

She revered the glory and majesty of God, of his care and compassion, and celebrated all of his creations. And she taught us to practice the faith in relation to fulfilling our personal sense of being and humanity. She would tell us, "Always stay close to God."

She had all seven children go to catechism classes from Kindergarten through high school. I was an altar boy and sang in the church choir. I taught catechism for years as a display of my care and passion of faith. I have been a lecturer and cantor in church. And I have been a Eucharistic Minister for most of my adult life. These are ways that I follow my mother's lessons of keeping God in my life—both for her and for myself.

• • •

My mother would tell me that the nature of my faith was not invalidated by my sexuality, though I should practice humility and respect in both. And despite some interpretive aspects of catholicity that might demonize my queer identity, my mother told me that a performed and enacted faith is not restricted by desire. It's measured by the character and practice of that faith in its most empowering and altruistic features.

• • •

There is an old joke based in what I call directional—or misdirectional—humor. You might know the joke. It goes like this: A New York City tourist, or maybe a young musician, asks a passerby: "How do you get to (the famed music venue) Carnegie Hall?"

And the answer is?

"Practice, Practice, Practice!"

And such is the answer to the question that I have been asked to respond to in my personal life.

> Question: How do you maintain your faith as a member of the LGBTQ+ community?

> Answer: Practice, Practice, Practice!

•••

For me, faith is not belief without proof. I believe that a credible faith is a rational faith that looks at the nature of being as evidence of knowing. The commitment to faith is a rhetoric of engagement, meaning that which we speak and on whose behalf we build arguments of defense and promotion. But also: that which we must embody and make manifest in our actions.

So, when I say and tell others:

> I believe in a God who is our loving Father and creator. And that God's love is limitless and overflows into our hearts and lives. And that God has created us out of His love that sustains and supports us daily. I then carry that with me in my daily life and in the choices that I make in my life. Being a member of the LGBTQ+ community does not offset that belief; in fact, I hope that my faith emboldens my identity in all the things that I do.

So, when I say and tell others:

> I believe that my faith to love God above all else and to love others is manifested in a practice of forgiveness, mercy, and commitment to care for the poor and helpless. That extends into my membership in the LGBTQ+ community and beyond. As a part of my faith, I practice and work for peace and justice in our world. This means that I am bringing God's kingdom of peace, unity, and love to a world faced with conflict, division, and strife through my embodied queer particularity, not in spite of it.

So, when I say and tell others:

> That my faith—LGBTQ+, embodied or otherwise—recognizes the need for forgiveness and sees the sacrament of reconciliation as a means to receive this great gift of God's forgiveness. That does not mean forgiveness for my queer identity, but forgiveness for the many failures and foibles of my humanity at large.

My faith requires and recognizes the importance of practiced prayer and daily critical reflection in both formal and informal ways, whether on my knees supplicating myself or negotiating the daily traffic behind the wheel of my car. An Examen by any other name is still prayerful contemplation. I also tell people that my faith recognizes the importance of service to others. Believing that Jesus came to serve and not to be served, I too strive to be more Jesus-like in my daily living.

Hence, the answer to the question, "How do you maintain your faith as a member of the LGBTQ+ community?" is: "Practice, Practice, Practice!" Having faith means being engaged in faith practices daily: in my scholarship, in my art, in my teaching, in my leadership, and the ways in which all of those meet in the confluence of everyday living.

• • •

But there is also another question that was asked of me:

> Question: How I do I maintain friends and relationships in my personal and professional life?

> Answer: Being consistent and fully present in myself, in my whole self, which includes my faith and queer identity among other things. It means making fully present all aspects of my complex intersectional identity:

as a man,
as Black/man,
as a Black/gay/man,
as a Black/gay/Catholic/man
as a Black/gay/Catholic/man/citizen/
as a Black/gay/Catholic/man/citizen/teacher/artist/scholar/
administrator/

as a Black/gay/Catholic/man/citizen/teacher/artist/scholar/administra-
tor/brother/
as my mother's son and my father's boy
and always as a child of God.

It means making my intersectional self fully and consistently present to
engage and help others—and the world—to recognize support and celebrate
our joint humanity while promoting justice.

This is most appropriately done through practices of information, formation, and transformation for self and others. It's fundamental to do so with
great PRIDE. Not just PRIDE as a political activist move and positional statement, as in, "We're here and we're queer!" although that is always important.
But also pride as a feeling of deep pleasure or satisfaction in the possibilities
derived from one's faith: a faith through God to continually ask for the grace to
stand with others, the poor and the suffering; to educate, heal, and recognize
the humanity of the stigmatized; and to work to liberate the oppressed, even
as I am also oppressed.

From a secular place, as Adrienne Rich suggests, "Pride is often born in the
place where we refuse to be victims, where we experience our own humanity
under pressure, where we understand that we are not the hateful projections
of others but intrinsically ourselves." Such recognition of self-worth exists in
spite of social derision. It allows us to begin to thrive in our personhood and to
assist others in their struggles.

I strongly believe in the importance of racial, ethnic, and gender diversity
within any academic and professional environment, as it contributes to not
only the diversity of presence but also the diversity of ideas that enrich the
human and humanizing experiences in everyday life. Such a stance is not
only about an open embrace and hospitality as a feature that distinguishes
the Catholic Academy; it is at the core of a performed catholicity of tolerance,
welcome, and enrichment of self and other.

•••

So, in my personal and professional life, I have never had to overcome any perceived challenges of being accepted for any individual part of my intersectional
identity, though oppression is always and already collective. Yet the fullness
of my person lives and thrives where those places and elements of my intersectional identity do not just meet, but overlap and co-inform one another,
drawing strength from diverging and converging histories of resistance. There,

such histories meet to synergize, energize, and fortify my being. The struggle is therefore not particular to one trait but is plural to my whole self. The survival of and within that struggle has established this the *fabulous* person that my mother once described me to be.

The challenges are most often not my own, alone, but rather the perceptions of others who must negotiate their own values, their own sense of what is appropriate in the range of human social behavior, their own practice regarding their humanity, and their own practice of their faith. And hopefully that is:

A faith that requires practiced acceptance of human difference.
A faith that is celebratory of the diversity of all human beings.
A faith that recognizes the diversity of all God's creations.
A faith that respects the power of God's love made manifest in their practice.
And a faith that does justice.

There is no hate in a faith that does justice.

• • •

So, in conclusion:

My mother used to tell me that I was made in the image of God.

My mother used to tell me that she saw a light and joy in me that could give comfort and care to others, and that it was my responsibility to do so.

My mother used to tell me to be consistently present in my whole self, in my whole person—but always to give thanks to God for the many gifts and particularities that he had bestowed upon me.

My mother used to tell me to honor my own spirit and to respect my mind and body.

My mother used to tell me that God does not make mistakes.

My mother used to also tell me to keep God in my life, not just as refuge in times of strife but to practice faith as a commitment to the possibilities and potentialities of God's great promise of redemption.

And that is what I attempt to do every day, being fully present in a faith that does justice—a faith that allows me to be fully present in the lives of others, and a faith that allows me to be fully present on my own personal journey of both being and becoming a child of God.

I do not use my many gifts or my particularities to beat down, demean, or shame others in any aspects of my personal or professional life. Sometimes that is perceived as a weakness. My mother would tell me that it is a sign of God' strength in me.

I am my mother's son.

And all my life my mother—and particularly in my realized, out gay identity—would say, "Keith is still a relatively good Catholic boy." The "still" served as a mindful qualification of her own strict catholicity that still supported her gay boy's commitment to his faith in relation to his particularity. It was a playful acknowledgment between the two of us. We both smiled when she said it.

• • •

On my desk in my home and work offices sits a picture of my parents. It is my favorite picture of them. In its, they are dancing in an embrace that they only pause for the photographic moment. In the photo, my father has his signature sunshades on to protect his always sensitive eyes. My mother looks directly into the camera lens with a full smile. I imagine that she is always looking at me and approving of the man that I have become.

I have faith that all the things that my mother told me are true. I try to practice that faith daily in the fullness of my identity, thereby authorizing others to do the same. That applies to both those with the same struggles and also those who presume the privileges and comforts of naming and shaming others, further marginalizing the presumed other and creating a schism in our joint humanity.

I tell my story through the critical practices of autoethnography, using my lived experience as a cultural terrain for close scrutiny and a critical reflexivity. Like the "pensive" of *Harry Potter* fame, the methodological approach is a technology of reviewing stored memories to see again what one has once seen—or felt—before. It means revisiting that experience critically, with the exactitude of artistic practice. Then, with courage and conviction, it requires sharing the process and product of that discovery to wider cultural, social, and political audiences as testimony and evidentiary knowledge. I do this not for you to code on that which is presented, but to help you and others to see the technique and technology as a methodology, so that you (they) can begin your (their) own process of sense making.

I practice the religion as an act of faith.
I perform faith as an act of generosity and restraint.

I strive to achieve my own possibility and potentiality of being and becoming, while trying to assist others on their journey.

These are all the same things that I wish for you—and more.

Notes

1 See Alexander (2020).
2 This piece was constructed and video-taped as a message to my faculty and staff, as college dean, in response to the nation's 2020 civil unrest and the activities of the Black Lives Matter movement in response to the police murder of George Floyd in Minneapolis, MN. The piece was also featured as Alexander (2020).
3 A variation of this piece was first written and presented at the First LMU LGBTQ+ Retreat thru LMU Catholic Ministry on January 27, 2018. A portion was included in my 2019 Dean's Convocation entitled, "CFA as Templates of Sociality: Critical and Creative Protocols of Engagement." The included section in that broader presentation was in partial solidarity with and response to the exhibition, "Confess: An Installation," by Trina McKillen. The installation comments on the clerical child abuse scandal in the Catholic Church, and at the time was exhibited at the Laband Art Gallery at the College of Communication and Fine Arts, LMU. Part of McKillen's journey to creating this exhibition was based on her mother's dismay and disillusionment with the increasing cases of clerical abuse.

I originally delivered this presentation on the shared birthdate of my mother, Velma Ray Bell Alexander, and my brother, Nathaniel Patrick Alexander. Both are now deceased. My brother died in 1995 from HIV/AIDS. My mother retired from being a pediatric nursing assistant to take care of my brother at home. After his death, my mother spoke at church functions about the relationship between faith, sexuality, and love; about HIV/AIDS education in the Black community; and about unmediated love of a mother for her child in faith.

A modified version of the piece is embedded in a longer essay entitled Alexander, B. K. (Chapter). "Dense particularities: Race, spirituality, and queer/quare intersectionalities" (Alexander, 2021, 18–44).

Courageous Conversations

Bryant Keith Alexander

Dear Mary,

When I read your following three shortly plays, "A Conversation in an Elevator," "A Conversation at a Bus Stop," and "A Conversation at a Black Lives Matter Rally," I was taken. I was taken by how the phrase "Courageous Conversations" has come into vogue as a reference to people acknowledging and coming together to talk about issues of bias. But maybe more importantly, it means people intentionally coming together to talk about issues of race and racism as conjoined constructions that lean themselves to relational biases—in other words, as the politically correct way to get at "racism." This combines with the potential of learning strategies to mitigate intentional and unintentional judgments and their problematic outcomes.

Some of that work is powerful in its theoretical framing and its careful negotiations of the "other" on either side of the racial divide. It creates a space that does not engender defense in the process of finding a truce of understanding, and this with the effort of establishing sustained changes in behavior and sustained performances of civility. But your short plays take me to a different place, or maybe they take me to the place differently. Most of that work on "Courageous Conversations" comes in the form of structured seminars with trained intercultural facilitators who mediate between issues, sides, politics, and organizational ethics.

But I am also interested in the ways in which everyday encounters—whether simulated or real—occur between people from differing backgrounds who are forced in time, space, and circumstance to confront each other authentically without mediations, and how they speak to the sensibility of critical everyday encounters and resolution tactics. I am interested in how the staying-in-it of the moment, whether through the confinement of circumstance or the true desire to communicate is evidence of everyday efforts. I am interested in how micro-conciliations—as opposed to microaggressions—also make possible meaningful transformations.

Moments of authentic encounter can open up spaces of possibility. In this sense, sometimes I want to move ever so slightly from the assumed performances of "courageousness" as extraordinary feats or dedication to staging

© BRYANT KEITH ALEXANDER, 2021 | DOI: 10.1163/9789004464858_012

"courageous conversations" as educational mandates in learning and professional contexts, as important as they are. Sometimes I want to move into the dramatizations of everyday life that show real people working it out.

These approaches are not antithetical and may, in fact, co-inform a common purpose when used in conjunction toward liberation. Hence for me, the following three short plays really foreground desperate circumstances that force particular characters to attend not only to each other, but to the very social constructions that make each party "the other" to one another in critical moments that bespeak the urgency of conciliation. Each scene, whether read or viewed as a performance, can be used to have "courageous conversations" from a literary artifact that dramatize everyday life, making potent the politics of difference that need to be resolved. While your characters are specifically named in a performative pedagogy, I would like to see cross racial casting, allowing the presumed "other" of the characters to be spoken through the material embodiment of the other. That way, each can experience what true courage feels like. Just a thought.

Bryant

Three Conversations

Mary E. Weems

A Conversation in an Elevator

Characters:

Marcy: Black woman, 20s, graduate student and social activist. Has just
             returned from "Black Lives Matter" Rally, wears "Black Lives Mat-
             ter" t-shirt, black jeans, rust-colored Timberland boots. She's car-
             rying a book bag filled with flyers and other things slung over her
             right arm.

Sandy: White woman, late 40s, dressed stylishly but comfortable in tai-
             lored black trousers, white silk blouse, low-heeled black pumps.
             She carries a large designer bag.

*(Setting: Elevator in high-rise apartment building in an upper-middle-class
neighborhood. Marcy lives there with her parents, both civil rights attorneys.
Sandy's there to visit her daughter, an up-and-coming comedienne. Marcy enters
elevator on first floor and stands in the front, dead center. Sounds of elevator moving, ending with "bell" sound signaling its arrival on the 2nd floor. Sandy enters,
silently steps around Marcy, and stands directly behind her. After a few moments,
Marcy, who's uncomfortable and on guard, moves to the right and back corner
wall of the elevator. Sandy remains in her position)*

Marcy: We have the whole elevator, why were you standing right behind
             me? *(Beat)*

(Sandy responds without turning around)

Sandy: Because this is where I stand.
Marcy: What you say?

(Silence)

Marcy: Sandy?

© MARY E. WEEMS, 2021 | DOI: 10.1163/9789004464858_013

(*Sound of door arriving at next floor. No one enters. Sound of door closing and moving to next floor. Marcy moves to position herself right behind Sandy, who continues to stand quietly as if she doesn't notice. Suddenly the elevator jolts to a stop, and both women are tossed forward, then backwards quickly as the elevator lights go off, then quickly come back on. Both women land on the floor against the back wall in opposite corners. Marcy turns to watch Sandy, who is looking in her purse for something. Then Marcy stands and begins to breathe quickly, looking up at the sky as if to God, then nervously approaching the control panel to push the emergency button, which is not working.*)

Marcy: Hey!!! Help!! Can anybody hear me? We're stuck in this goddamn thing. Help!! Help!! Hel—
Sandy: Calmly. Will you cut that out?

(*Marcy shouts*)

Marcy: What you say?
Sandy: I SAID would you cut that shit out, please?
Marcy: Or what?

(*Silence*)

(*Marcy drops her book bag on the ground like a gauntlet.*)

Marcy: Or what lady? What are you going to do if I don't?

(*Silence*)

Marcy: Hey! What's your problem? Do you notice we're stuck here? That the bell doesn't work?

(*Sandy goes back to looking in her purse*).

Marcy: What are you looking for?
Sandy: (*Beat*) My cell phone.

(*Marcy begins laughing nervously.*)

Marcy: Oh shit, that's right this is the 21st century. This might sound odd, but I may have been one of the last ones in my generation to get a cell phone and half the time I leave it somewhere, at home, in my car, in my locker at school, in the grad office desk and—

Sandy: And I get it—you don't have yours, right?

Marcy: (*Beat*) Nope. Do you?

(*Sandy goes back to digging in her purse for a few seconds and comes up with her cell phone.*)

Marcy: Thank God and two or three other white folks as my grandpa used to say!

Sandy: He did? Why did he 'used' to say that? Sounds racist to me. Why white folks?

Marcy: Racist? My grandfather sacrificed his whole life to fight against segregation and for integration. My parents who own an apartment in this building, became Civil Rights attorneys to continue 'his' fight...it's why Johnny Cochran's one of my heroes.

Sandy: Okay, sorry, I didn't mean to hurt your feelings.

Marcy: Trust me, you didn't. As for 'why' white folks? Why not white folks? (*Beat*) What are you doing in this building anyway? I've never seen you before.

Sandy: I'm here to visit my daughter Ariana. Have been living out of the country for a while. Will have to share your grandpa's saying with my daughter. You know when she was—

Marcy: Ma'am? Focus, focus here. Will you please dial 911 so we can get some help?

Sandy: Oh, okay. Sorry, but this isn't the first time I've been stuck in an elevator. Matter of fact, I remember the first time like—

Marcy: Ma'am? Please?

Sandy: Okay, okay.

(*Sandy types in her security code to open her phone, then dials 911. She waits a moment until she gets the message, "Service not available"*)

Sandy: Oh shit.

Marcy: Oh shit?! Oh, shit what? What's wrong?

Sandy: (*Beat*)Can't make a call right now. Phone reads 'service not available.'

Marcy: Goddamn it! See what I mean. All this fucking technology, all these ways to communicate and do they work when you really need them? Hell naw. Now what?

(*Before Sandy can answer, Marcy begins pacing the elevator. She tries to pry the doors open. When she can't, she starts screaming at the top of her lungs: a piercing sound designed to get someone's attention.*)

Marcy: Ahhhhhhhhhhhhhhhhhhhhhhhhhhhhhhhhhhhhh!!!!!!!!

(*Sandy covers her ears with her hands for a few seconds. Then gets up and slaps Marcy in the face to snap her out of it. Marcy immediately slaps her back and the two women stand facing each other. Marcy steps back to get ready to fight.*)

Sandy: Wait, wait a minute! I'm sorry, okay? Didn't know what else to do so—

Marcy: So, you decided to take a chance on your life and slap me.

(*Sandy starts laughing uncontrollably. After a few moments, Marcy joins her.*)

Marcy: Damn, did I just say that? Talk about melodrama. If mama was here, she'd be reminding me of what she's always said about me.

Sandy: Which is what?

Marcy: That my dramatic ass belongs on somebody's stage somewhere instead of always organizing about something.

Sandy: Really? That's funny.

Marcy: Why?

Sandy: Because my mother used to say the same thing about me when I was a child.

Marcy: Did she change her mind when you got grown.

Sandy: (*Beat*) No, she died.

Marcy: Sorry Ma'am.

Sandy: (*Holds out her hand.*) That's okay. My name's Sandy.

Marcy: Mine's Marcy. (*Beat*)

(*They both sit down on the floor facing each other silently for a few moments. Sandy picks up her phone to see if she can make a call.*)

Marcy: Is it working yet?

Sandy: No, it's not.

(*Marcy looks around nervously*)

Marcy: Okay, okay, so you said this wasn't your first time being stuck in an elevator.

Sandy:	True.
Marcy:	What happened the last time? What did you do?
Sandy:	(*Beat*) First let me ask you something.
Marcy:	What?
Sandy:	Why did you freak out when it first stopped?
Marcy:	Because I've always been afraid of two things that involve elevators.
Sandy:	Which are?
Marcy:	I'm afraid of being locked in or trapped and I'm scared of heights.
Sandy:	Oh. Sorry to—
Marcy:	Okay, okay, I already know you're sorry, Sandy. Tell me what's up. How long are we going to be stuck in this thing?
Sandy:	Well, fact is unless my phone starts working, we're going to have to wait until somebody complains about this elevator not arriving to the floor they push and—
Marcy:	And the problem is, this is just one of many elevators in this place, it's early afternoon on a work day and since I live here I 'know' that Mr. Anderson, the only one on duty at this time of day, takes his lunch hour right about now.
Sandy:	(*Beat*) So since right at this moment we are in fact stuck, I have an idea I'd like us to try.
Marcy:	What?

(*Sandy takes off her pumps, semi-crosses her legs, then reaches over to take both of Marcy's hands in hers.*)

Marcy:	This is not some crazy shit is it?
Sandy:	No. It's something I learned to do a long time ago in times of stress. I want to guide you through a meditation exercise. Now—

(*Marcy jerks her hands away and stands up.*)

Marcy:	Meditation? You crazy, I can't goddamn even think and you want my mind to relax, shit I—
Sandy:	Then what do *you* suggest we do, young lady? We have at least 30 minutes if not more to be stuck in here together, two strangers not on a train—
Marcy:	On a train, what?
Sandy:	Never mind. I'm referring to an old-old Alfred Hitchcock movie about two white guys who meet on a train. One is from old money but crazy as a loon—and

Marcy: Loon, what's that?

Sandy: It's a bird that—never mind, let me finish, the rich guy is crazy as hell and the other is a man mad at his wife. They have this brief conversation and at the end of it the crazy one thinks he and the sane guy have a pact. The rich guy will kill the other one's wife on condition that once he does, the married guy will kill the rich one's father—who he hates with all his heart. The nutcase has it all figured out—the perfect murder.

Marcy: Dang, so what happens?

Sandy: Well, since nothing people do is ever perfect. It doesn't work out. After the crazy one kills the other's wife during a moonlight boat ride at a local carnival, he contacts the married guy, tells him he's completed his part of the bargain and discovers that his so-called partner in crime thought it was all a joke.

Marcy: I bet Richie Rich wasn't laughing, though was he?

Sandy: No, he was furious, stalked the man, tried to get him to change his mind and when he wouldn't

(*Sandy stops speaking*)

Marcy: What happened?

Sandy: Not telling you. It would spoil an amazing movie I'm hoping you'll take the time to watch when we get out of here.

Marcy: Now you're reminding me of my mother.

Sandy: Why?

Marcy: Cause she's a long-time old movie fan and she loves Hitchcock, but—

Sandy: But what?

Marcy: She's never been able to get me to sit still long enough to watch anything in black and white, not even an old TV show, but now you've got my interest so—

Sandy: So, you'll get a copy and watch it?

Marcy: Yep, if we can ever get out of this elevator. It's a deal.

Sandy: How will I know?

Marcy: You kidding?

Sandy: Am I smiling?

Marcy: (*Beat*) Okay, it's obvious you're not. How can I reach you?

(*Sandy reaches into her purse and pulls out her business card case.*)

Sandy: Here's my card. Send me a text.
Marcy: Okay.
Sandy: Promise?
Marcy: Yep. Promise.

(*Marcy looks at her watch.*)

Marcy: We've been on this thing about 15 minutes. I'm starting to—
Sandy: So, I notice you're wearing a "Black Lives Matter" t-shirt.
Marcy: Yeah, what about it?
Sandy: (*Beat*) Not sure if I should pretend I give a shit about
           political correctness or just do my usual.
Marcy: Which is?
Sandy: Speak my mind as if I don't give a shit, when really, I do.
Marcy: What do you mean?
Sandy: I mean that since President Obama became president too many
           white folks and others are claiming this country, founded on the
           backs and lynched necks of Black slaves is post-racial. I mean
           that I'm sick to death of watching good people of all kinds who
           do care walk around holding their collective breath, afraid to say
           what's on their minds.
Marcy: (*Beat*) I agree. Why do you think that is?
Sandy: If I had the answer to that question, I'd be standing on the corner
           sharing with any and everybody that would listen to me.
Marcy: Okay, I get that, but you obviously have an opinion. What do you
           think?
Sandy: I think the answer is as not-simple as how race, culture, class,
           religion and etc. operate in a country filled with people who all
           want some of the same things and are doing their level best to
           live without dealing with their fear of any kind of difference.
Marcy: Yeah. (*Beat*) the 'D' word. Never thought about it quite like that,
           but even though I haven't lived as long as you—
Sandy: Oh really? How do you know how old I am?
Marcy: I don't but if I had to guess—
Sandy: Never mind about guessing. Let's just say I'm old enough to be
           your mother.
Marcy: Dang, is that all?
Sandy: Alright, let's get back to what you were about to say.

Marcy: (*Beat*) Both my mama and daddy are Civil Rights attorneys and
            God willing I'm going to be one too. Weird thing is my choice isn't
            based on my parents.

Sandy: Really? Not following in their footsteps. Then what?

Marcy: (*Beat*) Johnny Cochran's.

Sandy: Johnny Cochran's what?

Marcy: Footsteps, Ms. Sandy. I want to follow his lead. I want to take on
            major cases where it looks like the only possible verdict is guilty,
            I want to defend folks who can and can't afford to defend them-
            selves. I want to help innocent Black people fight a system that
            was designed to fail them. I want to—

Sandy: I think I get your point, but why Johnny Cochran in particular?
            There have been a number of Black Civil Rights lawyers—

Marcy: And my parents have made certain that I know who they are,
            but it's one thing to read about someone long dead or long ago
            retired and another altogether to have a chance to watch them in
            action. (*Beat*)

Sandy: True good point. But—

Marcy: Let me finish. The reason why Johnny Cochran's one of my heroes
            is because regardless of which side of the O.J. Simpson case you're
            on. That Black man gave that case all he had. He fought long, and
            hard, and consistently exhausting all possible avenues to get a
            man off because—

Sandy: Because he believed he was innocent?

Marcy: That's irrelevant in the law.

Sandy: Is it?

Marcy: It is in this sense. Under the law every human being has the right
            to a fair trial—period. (*Beat*) The reason Lady Justice is blind
            is because the law is not supposed to base its decisions on skin
            color, or class, or whether or not the jury likes a defendant.

Sandy: Yet, all of those things come into play, don't they?

Marcy: But they're not supposed to. I think Mr. Cochran was able to real-
            ize all of the shit that muddies the water of the truth and still
            fight for a person's right to a fair trial and bottom line, I still don't
            know if O.J. killed his wife and that dude, I just know the prose-
            cution didn't prove it beyond a reasonable doubt.

Sandy: What was that saying Cochran made up?

Marcy: If it doesn't fit, you must acquit. (*Beat*) I can still see him in that
            courtroom with that glove, pulling the jury's attention to it,

placing little pieces of doubt in their minds while they were staring, his sole focus getting his client a not-guilty verdict.

Sandy: (*Beat*) I think he was guilty.

Marcy: I don't care. (*Beat*) How's that for political correctness?

Sandy: Okay, I see your point.

Marcy: Do you? Then you'd be one of the few white people I've met today
or maybe ever who do.

Sandy: Meaning.

Marcy: Black Lives 'do' Matter (*Beat*) no matter what.

Sandy: I know.

Marcy: And just how do you know Sandy? What is I about your life that
makes you able to understand that?

Sandy: I—

Marcy: I mean, Goddamn. This country is, was, and always has been racist as what and every time I turn around a Black man is being
shot down like a dog by some cop who cares more about the life
of his police dog than a brother losing his life.

Sandy: Well I—

Marcy: Shit, me and too few people have been organizing, using our
phones for cop watching and Facebooking and cell phoning
and flyer passing and meeting and stopping traffic in the streets
for months and before we can finish protesting for one shooting another one's happening in another city somewhere and it's
damn near like starting all over again. (*Beat*) I'm tired.

Sandy: I understand—

Marcy: No, you don't, you're as clueless as the rest of the so-called majority that's really always been the minority in this world.

Sandy: What?

Marcy: What I mean is most of the world is not-white, so how can I be
a minority? Fact is, if you added up all the not-white people of
color including the legal and illegal immigrants if you could get
an accurate count, and lump them together like this government
lumps all the white folks together under "Caucasian" who would
be in the minority?

Sandy: (*Beat*) Never thought about it like that.

Marcy: You don't have to. You don't have to think about it at all.

Sandy: (*Beat*) What makes you so certain. You've never seen me before in
your life, and I've never seen you. What do we really know about
each other?

Marcy: Good point. (*Beat*) Okay, so tell me something about yourself. Do you have even one Black friend? And before you answer, please don't give me that bullshit about your best friend being Black?

Sandy: (*Beat*) Well, sorry to disappoint you but even if everybody you've ever heard say that was lying doesn't mean I am and the fact is—my best friend for over 25 years was and is Black and as she always reminds me when ignorant, racist shit happens—she's dark skinned too.

Marcy: (*Beat*) And what does her—dark, skin have to do with anything?

Sandy: Come on now, who's screwing with who? You know what I mean.

(*Silence*)

Sandy: I mean that it's one thing to be Black in America, but at least if you're light or what my friend calls "light, bright or damned near white" you somehow have it easier in this country, you're not so scary, you don't make white folks feel so uncomfortable.

Marcy: White folks like you?

Sandy: White folks who aren't like me. (*Beat*) You know all white people aren't the same anymore than—

Marcy: Okay, okay you know what I mean, 'most' white folks.

Sandy: Really? What are you basing that on? How many white folks do you know up close and personal?

Marcy: We aren't talking about me though, you were telling me about your best friend. So, tell me.

Sandy: Let me tell you a story about a couple of experiences she and I have had together. Maybe that will help.

(*Marcy looks around the elevator. She adjusts her body to a more comfortable seated position.*)

Marcy: Okay, I'm all ears. Tell me.

Sandy: My friend Claudia is an amazing writer. All of her books are about Black children, and all of her stories are read and loved by all kinds of kids all over the country, in other countries too.

Marcy: And?

Sandy: Claudia's always being invited to come to elementary schools, high schools, colleges, and conferences to read her work, sign books, and shake hands with her readers, but she doesn't drive.

	This means any time she has to go somewhere too close to fly or take the train—
Marcy:	What about the bus?
Sandy:	She hates buses. As I was saying, any time she has to go somewhere within driving distance, I drive her and she pays me to help her. (*Beat*) The strange thing is and we've talked about this so many times, now we just give each other a look when it happens, even though everybody who hires her should know she's Black and I'm obviously not, they always think "I'm" the writer and she's my helper. Claudia calls it the 'maid' syndrome.
Marcy:	Dang, really?
Sandy:	Who could make something like this up? Yes, every single time I take her any place, I always have to tell people that Claudia's the famous writer and that I'm her friend. (*Beat*) It used to really bother her and make me feel like I was part of the reason they thought this, but after learning from her about some of the things too many white people don't know or care to know—I think I get it. I don't like it, fact is I hate it, but as Claudia says—when you're Black and dark, all white people can see when they look at you is Mammy. It's like living in the "Gone with the Wind" movie, you never get out of the kitchen in the white imagination and you can never be the smart one or the talented one or the accomplished one when you show up with somebody white by your side.
Marcy:	Damn straight. That's always been true.
Sandy:	(*Beat*) Claudia and I are both Democrats and every time there's an election coming up, we work together at the local office making cold calls, creating and passing out flyers, cleaning up after hours, whatever's needed. Well, one night I was seated at one of the work tables stuffing flyers and Claudia was busy sweeping the floor so we could get out of there before our usual 11 o'clock. We'd forgotten to lock the door and one of the wealthy members of our community waltzed in to see if there was anything she could do now that she knew the work had been done, you know, pretending that if there was work to be done, she'd actually do something besides make a large donation to our party. Claudia and I gave each other a look behind her back and I offered to get her some coffee. We were both hoping she'd say no and get out but no such luck. (Beat) After I got her coffee, gave it to her and continued with what I was doing. I noticed her watching Claudia

sweep. All of sudden I heard her say "You missed a spot over there, you need to go back over it."

Marcy: Dang.

Sandy: (*Beat*) I sat there holding my breath. Claudia continued to sweep as if she hadn't heard her.

Marcy: And when was this, a long time ago?

Sandy: It was last year. (*Beat*) After a few minutes, I heard the woman who Claudia still calls an 'ignorant-white-bitch' to this day as if it's her name say, "Excuse me girl, but did you hear what I said?" Claudia continued to sweep as the woman raised her voice "Are you deaf? Did you hear what I said?" Claudia stopped sweeping, turned to look at the woman with the broom in her hand. She stood there so long, while I sat there like a mute ass unable to utter a word, that the idiot finally got up in a huff, dropped her empty Styrofoam cup on the floor and said, "You're lucky you don't work for me or you'd be fired!"

(*Before Marcy can respond, they hear the voice of Mr. Anderson coming from the ceiling*)

Voiceover: Hey! Who's in there? Anybody stuck?

Marcy: Yeah, we are! It's me Marcy, Mr. Anderson, please help us, me and another woman have been trapped in here for over an hour.

Voiceover: Alright Ms. Marcy, I'll be right down. I can tell the two of you are stuck between a rock and a hard—err I mean the 3rd and 4th floors. Hang in there now, I'll be right down. It should start moving any moment.

(*Marcy and Sandy look at each other for a few moments.*)

Sandy: Don't forget to watch that movie.

Marcy: I won't Ma'am. Strangers on a Train, right?

Sandy: Directed by Alfred Hitchcock. You have my card. Text me and maybe we can meet for coffee to talk about it.

Marcy: Okay, I will.

(*Stage to black as audience hears the sound of the elevator beginning to move.*)

The End

A Conversation at a Bus Stop

Characters:

Michael: Black man, early 30s
Matt: White man, late 50s

(*Setting: A city bus stop facing the street. It's Saturday, and a Black man wearing headphones walks down the street in rhythm to the music he's listening to, rapping. He enters the bus stop and takes a seat at the far end, noticing a white man wearing navy work pants, a white t-shirt and black work shoes sitting on the opposite end of the bench reading the newspaper. The Black man is immediately on his guard, not only because the man is white, but because he's never seen a white man in this bus stop in his neighborhood.*)

(*Michael sees someone exchange weed and money across the street. He talks to himself loudly enough for Matt to hear.*)

Michael: Damn, that's all I see around here since I've been home.

(*Matt continues reading his paper.*)
(*Michael's cell phone rings.*)

Michael: Hello? Ma? Yeah, I'm on my way to your house now. Waiting for the number 1. What's up? What? Wait a minute, wait a minute mama, slow down so I can hear you. Come on now stop! No, I'm not hollerin' at you, I'm trying to get you to tell me what happened.

(*He listens for a moment, drops his head, speaks quietly.*)

Michael: Yeah, I understand everything you said. Right now, I don't know what to say, we'll talk. Yes, mama, I'm comin' as fast as I can. You know how the bus works around here, it gets here when it gets ready and these drivers will drive off and leave your ass, sorry ma, leave your behind, if they even think you gon' give them some trouble. Okay, see you soon.

(*Matt folds his paper back into shape, puts it under his arm, and looks out to see if the bus is on the way. Michael keeps a careful eye on him, trying to feel out what*

*he's doing here. Matt takes out his phone and begins sending someone a long text
as Michael takes out a cigarette, stands beside the bus shelter, lights it, and takes
a puff or two. Just before Matt finishes his text, a fast car drives by, hits the standing water in front of the bus stop and drenches Matt's pants and shoes from about
the knee down. Michael immediately starts laughing, and Matt turns around.)*

Michael: Ooops! Sorry, not laughing 'at' you, just laughing 'cause that shit
                was funny.

(Matt takes a rag out of his pocket and starts blotting up the water.)

Matt: Was it? You always laugh when—okay, okay, it was funny.

*(Michael relaxes a bit, steps back inside the shelter and takes his seat at the other
end.)*

Matt: How much longer before 'any' bus comes this way? I've been
                waiting so long; I'll even take a wrong bus.
Michael: I feel you, but you might as well relax. We got at least another 20
                minutes, maybe more.

(Matt takes his bus schedule out of his pocket.)

Matt: So it sounds like I may as well throw this thing away huh?
Michael: Naw, when you get up outta this part of town, the CTA runs a little
                better. You might even catch a bus or two on schedule. If you do,
                take a picture.
Matt: Come on now it can't be that bad.
Michael: You're right. Truth is I know a lot of bus drivers and most of them
                are doing their best to be on time every time. Problem is—
Matt: I suspect the problem is life. The unexpected things that happen
                to slow a bus down.
Michael: Good point. Come to think about it. I've been riding the bus since
                I was about 8 years old and I've seen a lot of those unexpected
                things you're talkin' about.
Matt: You have? Like what for example?
Michael: One time, I was on the one trying to get home after work. The bus
                was packed. It was about 5:30 in the evening and everybody and
                they mama was tryin' to get home from wherever they'd been.
                A lot of people were standing too 'and' it was one of the hottest

July's we'd ever had. People were literally wearing sweat like it was part of their outfit. This real dark and lovely was standing—

(*Sounds of an emergency vehicle interrupt Michael. Matt puts down his newspaper between them on the bench and leans forward to listen more closely. Michael takes a moment to watch the emergency vehicle rush down the street. He crosses himself.*)

Michael: Hope everybody's alright.

(*Silence*)

Michael: Anyway, like I was sayin' this tall dark and lovely Black woman was standing about two people up from me. Her belly was so big people were standing around it, asking her stuff like when's the baby due and if she knew what it was gon' be and all of sudden she started screamin' "My water broke, my water broke, I ain't due until—." Before she could finish her sentence, people had made a place for her to lie down, they were usin' soft book bags, head wraps, fast food workers were takin' off their aprons, anything to make some kind of pallet. Meantime, I ran up front and told the bus driver what was goin' on. She immediately found a safe place to stop the bus, got on her radio and called the po-lice, then—

(*Michael's phone rings. He holds up his hand to Matt and stops to answer it.*)

Michael   Hello? Who is this? Naw, you must have the wrong number. Huh? You whose cousin. Tommy's?

(*Michael listens for a few moments.*)

Michael: Oh, okay, I got who you are now. You Tommy's little cousin. One that used to live in Atlanta. Yeah, the cute one. Naw, I don't mean no disrespect, sorry about that.

(*Michael listens, begins looking sadder, holds his head down and lowers his voice.*)

Michael: I know, I know. He still hangin' in there. Good, good to hear, ma made it sound like, yeah, sure you right, she does blow shit up sometimes before it needs to be a bomb. I'm on the way Carla, meet you at mama's house. Hope you know I love dude like a brother. Okay, peace.

(Matt is standing in front of the bus stop pretending to read part of the paper and had turned away from Michael to give him a little privacy.)

Michael:	Sorry about that I—
Matt:	That's okay. One thing about cell phones, you're never more than a phone call away.
Michael:	No lie.
Matt:	Not like it was when I was growing up.
Michael:	Yeah Ma Bell and something called pay phones.
Matt:	What do you know about pay phones?
Michael:	I know the phone company got tired of crackheads robbing the ones in my neighborhoods so they stopped fixin' them, but left the guts standing all over my streets like broke sentinels.
Matt:	So what happened on that bus and how long ago was it?
Michael:	Don't remember exactly when. Time flies so fast—
Matt:	Aren't you a little young to feel like that? When I was your age—
Michael:	And how old is that?
Matt:	A helluva lot older than you are.
Michael:	Okay, you got me there. When you were my age what?
Matt:	Time took forever. Days seemed twice as long as they do now.
Michael:	You were lucky to feel like that. I can't remember a time I didn't think it was flying so fast, I'd never catch it until I was dead.
Matt:	Dead's something I know a lot about, but—
Michael:	But what?
Matt:	But we weren't talking about death, I was caught up in the story you were telling. Will you finish before something else interrupts us?
Michael:	Definitely. So, next thing was I asked if anybody on the bus knew anything about babies and an old woman sittin' way in the back passed the word up that she'd been a midwife in the South most of her life.
Matt:	Sheez! What are the odds of that happening?
Michael:	Probably one in a billion but believe me, we weren't thinking about anything but being grateful she was on that bus. We got out of her way and I watched as everything I thought I knew about having babies turned into a lie.
Matt:	What do you mean?

Michael: Have you ever seen a baby born?

Matt: Yes, my son and my daughter.

Michael: Were they on a bus?

Matt: Then you don't know what I'm talking about.

Michael: That old woman started working with the mother. Talking soft
            and low to her, massaging her legs, telling her to get up on all
            fours. She took over like a drill sargeant in a boot camp when
            it came to us too. Telling us to stay back, be quiet, turn off our
            devices and pay attention. (*Beat*) Well, before we knew it, we
            could see this bloody circle of hair appear between her legs, she
            was screaming and pushing, deep breathing and pushing, pray-
            ing and pushing and then as if God slapped her on the butt that
            baby came out into the world, the midwife stuck her finger in her
            mouth and I heard the most beautiful sound I've heard before or
            since, new life—a girl.

(*Matt is weeping silently. It scares Michael.*)

Michael: Man, what happened. Did I say something wrong? Why you
            cryin'?

(*Silence*)

(*Matt unfolds and refolds the paper. Puts it under his arm. Stares off in front of
him as if Michael hasn't spoken. They sit silently for several moments.*)

Michael: By the time the ambulance got there, the cord was cut, the baby
            was cleaned up and somebody had wrapped her in this piece of
            African cloth one of the women had on her head. We found out
            the midwife's name was Sarah Mae and that's what the mother,
            Shaniqua decided to name her baby to honor the first hands that
            had touched her after God's.

Matt: Is this a true story? All of it?

Michael: Course. You can't make this kind of shit up. Plus, why would I?

Matt: I don't know. You don't know me from Adam. You could just be a
            good storyteller pulling my leg while we wait for this bus.

Michael: Okay, okay, you got a point there. My point is though—it's the
            gospel. I lived every word of it. Matter of fact, I think the reason
            I can't remember the exact year is because I was so scared some-
            thin' was gon' go wrong and stop that baby from being born right,

I don't think I took a real breath until they took mama and baby off that bus. (*Beat*) Matter of fact, look.

(*Michael takes his book bag from his back and points to a patch of olive oil.*)
(*Matt leans over to look.*)

Matt:	What? I don't see anything.
Michael:	Member I told you people used anything soft they had to prepare a place for her to give birth?
Matt:	Yes, so?
Michael:	So, the sista must have just oiled her hair that day because, when I put my book back under her head, she sweated so bad during labor, she left this patch of olive oil on my bag. Guess it is kinda faded by now, but every time I look at this spot the memory comes back just like it was yesterday.
Matt:	(*Beat*) Why have you been riding the bus all of your life? Didn't you ever learn to drive?

(*Matt looks around as if for a hidden camera.*)

Michael:	What's this some kinda new game show? Did I get picked for a new reality TV show about Black men who ride the bus or what?
Matt:	Of course not. Are you kidding?
Michael:	Yep. Definitely.
Matt:	So, why do you always ride the bus?
Michael:	Because on the first day of summer, the year I turned eight my mother was killed by a drunk driver. (*Beat*) She was standing at the bus stop under my grandmother's window. She'd just left from takin' care of my granny who was dyin' from cancer. (*Beat*) Drunk ran up on the curb, hit her so hard he cut her legs off just below the torso. (Beat) I didn't find this out until I turned 18. Coffin was closed at her funeral and me and my 5 brothers thought she'd been buried whole. (Beat) Man went to trial. Got forever in jail since he'd been busted too many times drunk driving before. And me—

(*Matt scoots over a little closer and puts his hand on Michael's shoulder.*)

Matt:	I'm terribly sorry you lost your mother this way young man.

(*Michael slowly removes his hand.*)

Michael: (*Beat*) My name's Michael.

(*Matt holds out his hand.*)

Matt: Matt, Matt John.
Michael: Matt John? Now who's lyin'? Who'd name their son Matt John?
Matt: Well there's no long story here. John is the family name or what
                it was turned into when my ancestors arrived from wherever we
                came from, and Matt or Matthew was my dad's name.
Michael: My whole life changed after we lost mama. Daddy'd died a couple
                years before over in the Middle East and nobody in the family
                could take six boys, so we were broken up and raised by a combi-
                nation of family members and strangers through the foster care
                system.
Matt: But I thought I heard you talking to your mother on the phone.
Michael: That's my play mama Ms. Johnson. She's been a foster parent for
                a long time and has probably raised more of somebody else's kids
                than the seven she gave birth to. Thanks to her I didn't even have
                to move out of the neighborhood. She came to mama's funeral,
                spoke to my auntie who took my brothers Joe and Marky and told
                her she wanted to raise me, that she'd get the paperwork straight-
                ened out.
Matt: And that's all there was to it?
Michael: Far as I know. That's the way it was explained to me anyway.
Matt: Alright, but what does this have to do with why you don't drive?
Michael: Not sure. All I know is when it came time for me to take driver's
                ed in school, I kept throwing up on the instructor.
Matt: What?
Michael: That's how Ms. Johnsons started every conversation with my
                instructor when he called. What? (*Beat*) Then she'd try every-
                thing. First, she tried coaxing me with words of encouragement,
                next making my favorite food each week when it was lesson time,
                next she came up to the school and beat my ass in front of the
                class, but nothing helped. Every time I get anywhere near a steer-
                ing wheel, I can't breathe and whatever I have in my stomach is
                up out of me and all over the car, my clothes everything before I
                say a word to my poor instructor.

Matt: (*Beat*) Damn. Do you think it has anything to do with how you
             lost your mom?
Michael: To do? Like what, what you mean?
Matt: I mean that since a car killed your mom—
Michael: You mean a stankin' drunk ass man killed my mama.
Matt: You know what I mean. Maybe unconsciously you're afraid of
             cars. Afraid something bad will happen if you drive.
Michael: I don't know about all that, but I know I had to get special permis-
             sion to graduate without it and since then, I catch the bus.
Matt: Do you think you'll ever learn to drive?
Michael: No. And mainly cause I don't want to. To me a car is to go from
             point A to point B and so far, I've managed to do just fine without
             one and without analyzing the hell out of why.
Matt: No problem. Don't mean to pry. It just that, for my generation—
Michael: What generation? You sound like that pop commercial.
Matt: No, Michael—not the Pepsi generation. Ever heard of the Baby
             Boomers?
Michael: Uhhhh—no.
Matt: Good because I'm right after it and if we ever had a name, I don't
             remember it. What I'm trying to say is, when I was coming up, I
             couldn't wait to learn to drive. If you wanted a cute girlfriend, to
             be popular at 'any' level you had to at least have a driver's license
             and 'access' to a car if you didn't own one.
Michael: Access? You mean like borrowing somebody's car?
Matt: Exactly. In my case it was my dad's second car.
Michael: Second car, damn. Must be nice. Sounds like your folks had at
             least 'some' extra money.
Matt: I don't know about all of that, but my father worked two full time
             jobs, and my mother was a police officer.
Michael: A po-lice officer. Your mama?
Matt: You mean my 'mother'—show respect and yes, my mother was a
             police officer.
Michael: What do you mean was? Is she still with you?
Matt: No.
Michael: What happened to her?

(*Silence*).

Michael: Matt?

Matt:	You were talking earlier about your whole life changing when you lost your mother.
Michael:	Yep.
Matt:	Me and my little brother's life changed, but differently.
Michael:	What you mean?
Matt:	Instead of happening all at once in a rush, like that woman's water broke. It was more like leaks in a house.
Michael:	Okay, but what happened man.
Matt:	Actually, my mother was and is still a police officer. She's not with me and my brothers, but she's not dead either.
Michael:	You have all brothers too.
Matt:	Yea, but not as many as you.
Michael:	Damn, getting stuff out of you is like pullin' teeth. Will you put some sentences together and tell me what the hell happened to y'all?
Matt:	My dad used to beat my mother. (*Beat*) Started after he lost his supervisor's job at the steel mill when it closed. At that time, she was a stay at home mother, taking care of me and my brother. After he lost his job, she found out the police department was looking for female police officers. Instead of talking it over with my dad, she just went and filled out the paperwork. She told me much later that she didn't think she was going to be called and didn't want to argue with my dad unless she had a reason too.
Michael:	I know that's right.
Matt:	Turns out she had a real talent for police work. Not only was she called, she finished the Police Academy at the top of her class and in no time, she was out on the streets with her Black male partner.
Michael:	How'd your dad take it?
Matt:	That's what's so weird. As far as I know, he never said a word to her about it. He took care of us after school while she was training and did all he could, even with the house work. Then one day. Me and my brother came home from school and instead of a hot meal, there was a note on the kitchen table addressed to our mother. (*Beat*) Never found out what it said, but not long after that my mother started dating her partner Charles.
Michael:	Damn, so you had a Black man spending time with your mother. How'd you feel about that?
Matt:	At first me and my little brother Ryan hated it. We wanted our dad back and we wouldn't even speak to the guy. But then—
Michael:	Your mother whipped y'all's behind?

Matt: No, then we met his son Rodney. (*Beat*) Rodney was one year younger than me and five years older than my brother. I'll never forget the first time Charles brought him over. He walked in our house like he'd always lived there with this big smile on his face and said "Hi I'm Black and it don't rub off so get used to it." (*Beat*) For some reason that struck me and my brother as funny and before I knew it, we were both falling out on the floor laughing. (*Beat*) Didn't take long before we were best friends. One day after he'd whipped my butt at chess after an extra-long game, I blurted out that he was the brother I never had. Not that I didn't love my little brother—there's just something between me and Rodney that's deeper than blood somehow.

Michael: Shit, sounds like this is heading for a fairy tale ending. Everybody getting along, Black dude as a brother, your mother in love with his father, his father in love with your mother. What happened? Did they get married?

(*Silence*)

Michael: Matt?

Matt: Almost. My mother and Charles spent as much time as they could together at work and after work at our house, or at Charles' house. Charles lived on the westside though and since he only had Rodney and my mom had to haul two kids around, we usually wound up at our house. (*Beat*) One time Charles had lost his spare key and it was almost dark when he got to our house. He thought me and my brother would be waiting for him, but we'd decided to go to the store planning to get back before he got there. (*Beat*) Charles knew my mom left the window to her room unlocked so he went to the back of the house to let himself in.

Michael: Damn you tell a story slow. Okay, so what happened?

Matt: Not sure who, but a neighbor called the police and told them there was some strange N-word trying to break in our house. (*Beat*) From what we were told, in minutes the house was surrounded with cops. Charles, the best thing that ever happened to my mom, was startled and turned around and threw up his hands to try to surrender. (*Beat*) To this day we really don't understand how it happened, but one of the cops started shooting and he wound up riddled with bullets in our back yard.

(*Michael puts his hand on Matt's shoulder. They sit this way for a few moments.*)

Michael:	Lord have mercy Matt. Did he die?
Matt:	Yes.
Michael:	I'm so sorry man. That's sad and wrong as hell. Did the cops go to jail?
Matt:	No. My mom and Charles' family did everything they could. She had the full support of her department, so a full investigation was made, there was a long trial, but at the end of the day the all-white jury decided they'd made a terrible mistake and they were all found not guilty.
Michael:	Damn.
Matt:	My mother couldn't live here anymore and took me my little brother and Rodney to Atlanta. She found another job with the police department and now she's a detective.
Michael:	So, what are you doing here?
Matt:	My little brother loved Atlanta, but me and Rodney hated it and couldn't wait to come back home as soon as we could.
Michael:	And?
Matt:	(*Beat*) And I'm on my way to the westside to the duplex me, my brother Rodney and our wives and kids share together.
Michael:	Damn for real?
Matt:	For real young man. You think I could make this shit up?

(*They hear the bus approaching as Michael phone rings.*)
(*Michael answers while he looks to see that it's his bus approaching.*)

Michael: Hello? Ma? Bus is just pullin' up. I'll be there in about 20 minutes. Okay, bye.

(*Matt reaches out to shake his hand, but Michael quickly embraces him before he gets on the bus. Matt returns to his seat to wait.*)

The End

A Conversation at a Black Lives Matter March

Characters:

DaRonda: Black woman, mid-to-late 20s. She is one of the main Black Lives Matter organizers and lives in the city where the protests are being held.

John: White man, late 60s to early 70s. Lifetime, Republican conservative, and a Trump supporter, he lives in a small Midwestern town and travelled to the city to participate in the march.

(Setting: Any major city in the United States. Use sound effects to give the sense that the streets are filled with people on both sides of the street. Two people march toward each other. A young Black woman marches in from the right side of the stage wearing an "I Still Can't Breathe T-Shirt" and carrying a large white sign that reads "Black Lives Matter." An elderly white man dressed in black pants, a white shirt, and a red MAGA hat marches in from the left carrying a large white sign that reads "All Lives Matter.")

DaRonda: *(Shouts)* Black lives matter, Black lives matter, Black lives matter...
John: *(Shouts)* All lives matter, all lives matter, all lives matter...

(They continue chanting and holding their signs above their heads until they are too close to take another step.)

(John drops the sign to block his face with one hand and sticks his other hand straight in front of him to block DaRonda from getting any closer.)

John: Stop! Don't touch me.

(DaRonda drops her sign and lets it rest on the ground.)

DaRonda: Don't touch you? Are you kidding? What makes you think I want to touch you, white man?
John: Because you were shouting, moving toward me quickly, and I didn't know what to expect.
DaRonda: And I didn't either.

(The two stand face-to-face for a few seconds in silence.)

John: Why are you and your people insisting on talking about Black peoples' lives mattering?
DaRonda: How much time you got?

(John gets her point and relaxes a bit.)

John: Okay, okay, young woman, I think I'm beginning to get your point.

DaRonda:	Good, because I've been out here almost a month and I can't tell you how many white folks I've heard get pissed off because me and my fellow protestors want Black lives to matter in this country.
John:	Why do you think some of us are upset?
DaRonda:	I have an opinion, but since you're here, with a sign, protesting my being here, why don't you tell me?
John:	Right. Well, I can't speak for every white person in America, and wouldn't exactly say I'm angry about it, but I am confused.
DaRonda:	Confused about what?
John:	Because when my ancestors, immigrated here for a better life in 1922—

(*DaRonda interrupts*)

DaRonda:	From where?
John:	Northern Italy. I'm Italian American. As I was saying, when my ancestors left Venice, they didn't have much more than the shirts on their backs, a few coins in their pockets and the address of a Catholic family willing to take them in and help them get on their feet.
DaRonda:	Damn. I grew up poor, but we've never been that broke. How'd your folks get here?
John:	In the steerage area of a big ship.
DaRonda:	Kind of like the Titanic?
John:	Worse...from stories passed down to my father, people traveling in steerage were treated just a little better than the animals that part of the ship was made for. All they wanted to do was get to America, where they'd been told the streets were paved with gold and life for anyone who made it would be easy.
DaRonda:	From what I know about history, I'm guessing "easy" was a big overstatement.
John:	Yes, it was. They endured a lot, especially after my great-great-great grandfather found a job and we moved to New York... crowded living, they didn't speak a word of English.
DaRonda:	I know about crowded living. Mama had ten of us, we lived in a 2-bedroom apartment, with roaches running the walls each month when the exterminator sprayed, and never enough food. I didn't have my own bed, let a-lone room, till I got grown and moved out. How'd your family learn to speak English? That must have been hard as hell.

John: I'm sure it was. I don't actually know how they learned. That part
            of the story wasn't passed down, but I do know it took a while,
            all they wanted to do was see how fast they could assimilate into
            this country, work hard and get even a little piece of the Ameri-
            can Dream.

DaRonda: You mean nightmare?

John: No, I mean dream...It took a while, but a couple generations later,
            Giuseppe became John, the Italian flag was replaced by a proud
            American Flag outside of every one of our homes, and all of us
            were successful in some kind of trade.

DaRonda: What do you mean, like carpenters, plumbers?

John: That's right. Carpenters, plumbers, brick layers, iron workers. The
            kind of jobs that pay well, became unionized for better working
            conditions and so on.

DaRonda: So, it's obvious your people like mine have experienced serious
            struggle and at least some prejudice, what is it you don't under-
            stand about the Black Lives Matter movement?

John: I don't understand why Black people, after going through centu-
            ries of slavery and oppression, don't just stop focusing on their
            skin color and work harder to be accepted as Americans, period.

(*DaRonda picks up her sign and prepares to leave*)

DaRonda: Thanks, for explaining how you feel and why you're out here, but
            if you don't understand that after what's happened in these last
            few months, which is what's been happening to us for four hun-
            dred and one years, the rest of my life wouldn't be enough time
            to explain it to you...Glad we met, appreciate your story. Take it
            easy.

(*John extends his hand, and DaRonda leans forward to shake it before she turns
to raise her sign, walk toward her group.*)

DaRonda: Black lives matter! Black lives matter! Black lives matter!

(*DaRonda continues her chant until she's off stage, while John watches her as he
takes off his MAGA hat and stands with his sign turned toward his leg by his side.*)

The End

Trigger Warnings

Bryant Keith Alexander

Dear Mary,

"Trigger warnings" are statements at the start of a public communication—spoken, written, or film—designed to alert the audience, reader, or viewer that upcoming content or subject matter may contain potentially distressing material. Maybe like the use of strong language, adult content, disturbing visual imagery, etc., they are intended as a form of psychological brace for what some might find disarming. I agree with the sentiment. So, I am offering such a trigger warning for the following pieces relative to a particular performance of outrage and the use of the word "fuck"—repeatedly. The outrage and the use of the "F-word" are contextualized.

But sometimes I feel bereft at the need to warn others, as a courtesy that I don't often receive—that Black people don't often receive. I feel bereft at the fact that so many Black folks don't receive a "trigger warning" when our humanity is charged and our lives and livelihood are threatened by racist epitaphs, by actual guns, by a knee to the neck that threatens and succeeds in suffocation. When our bodies are stopped while driving Black, or our bodies are snatched off the public streets and hung. I even feel bereft at how the specter of our images are used to perpetuate hate for personal gain—both the dramatic and the banal—as cumulative and daily microaggressions on our persons wash over us like white noise. Such microaggressions lead to assaults on our humanity and our bodies, and sometimes they come not just from White folks. Sometimes the tools of the master can be appropriated for personal gains from within.

We all need trigger warnings to protect not just our sensibilities and hurt feelings, but to protect our very lives. We need them long before the gun is fired or the sentence announced, long before they find our bodies hanging. Hanging from ropes or attached to horrific intrusions into our daily domesticity, proving once again that none of us are safe: brothers, sisters, and those who live in-between. All of our bodies are on the line—one way or another.

Bryant

© BRYANT KEITH ALEXANDER, 2021 | DOI: 10.1163/9789004464858_014

Bamboozled

Mary E. Weems

Dear Bryant,

As a lifelong ally of the LGBTQ+ community, I was immediately outraged by what I'd heard had happened to Jussie Smollett. I tried to feel what it was like to be attacked for being Black and gay on a colder-than-hell late night walk for a sandwich. Smollett's description of what happened to him—the homophobic name calling, the noose, the violence immediately—triggered my need to write about what he suffered. When the truth was revealed a short time later, I felt completely what Malcolm X first called "bamboozled," tricked, made a fool of. And for what?

Mary

CHAPTER 9

Eat Fresh

Mary E. Weems

*Jussie Smollett, attacked outside a Subway for being Gay and Black
January, 2018*

Ice-cold winter night. Nineteen starting like eighteen ended, unpredictable weather pushed by climate change. This night taking Jessie back to his little boy years when his small mittened hand was held by a mama who never let him get more than a foot away. J as his closest friends called him was gay, Black and the kind of fine that needed nothing more than soap, water and clean clothes. God had hooked him up and even better, he was unaware of it. After a long day at his office job and an evening spent auditioning, then networking, he was hungry, but wanted something he didn't have to cook, especially at 2 o'clock in the morning.

Riding in the back of a cab with an old-man-driver so quiet he wanted to check his pulse, J looked to the left and saw an all-night Subway a few blocks from his apartment. He stopped the cab, paid the driver, deciding to walk home, he crossed the street to enter. "MAGA faggot!" He stopped quick, looked to his right too late to stop the two white fists from punching him in the face from both sides so fast Jessie dropped like a cut puppet, the blows coming hard like hail, muffled sounds of cars passing, the white men screaming "NIGGER, FAGGOT, FUCK YOU, OUR COUNTRY, MAGA MOTHERFUCKER..." Then something wet poured from the one standing over him, the other straddled, holding him down. They beat him till they got tired...walking slowly away shouting "THIS MAGA COUNTRY, BITCH"

Bleeding from his cracked mouth, nose, his ears ringing, he laid there until he couldn't hear a sound...crawled to the curb, using the edge to stand. He felt himself walk too long to the doors of the hospital's emergency room, collapsing in the attendant's arms.

Tomorrow. J's okay considering—has posted on Instagram. Black, gay, proud, defiant as ever. The news retelling a story older than time: Unidentified white men, no camera footage of them, no suspects, someone said the men were wearing red MAGA hats, but this has not been confirmed—we're back after this word from Subway.

CHAPTER 10

Not a Fan Letter

Or, Trigger Warning: An Autoethnographic Rant on Jussie Smollett

Bryant Keith Alexander

Dear Jussie Smollett,[1]

As one Black gay man living in America to another;

As one Black gay man living and struggling in a country still rife with racism, sexism, and gender bias to another;

As one Black gay man living in America where Black males are still suspect on the highways and byways of our daily travels; where police, white or otherwise, are killing us as ritual play, and our cries—and those of our spouses, parents, partners, and children—remain unheard (Black Lives Matter)[2];

As one Black gay man living in a *dream deferred,* in a nation where the *color of our skin and not the content of our character* is still the mainstay of our existence[3];

As one Black gay man living in a country where my sexuality is presumed antithetical to my masculinity and is still held suspect in some aspects of the Black community;

As one Black gay man who has achieved some level of personal and professional recognition, and who knows by near-daily experiences that the materiality of my presence often precedes the perception of my intellect;

I am taken back by your strategic carelessness which further makes us suspect all the time.

As one Black gay man living and dying in America to another, let me just say, "Fuck you!"

Fuck you for filing a false police report claiming you were the victim of a hate crime carried out by two assailants on a city street in Chicago.[4]

© BRYANT KEITH ALEXANDER, 2021 | DOI: 10.1163/9789004464858_017

Fuck you for your *empire of terror* on the City of Chicago when you claimed that the two masked men hurled racist and homophobic slurs before beating you and pouring what you believed was bleach over you and put a noose around your neck in your upscale neighborhood. [5]

You are *not* Emmett Till, who was killed after being accused of offending—nay looking, whistling at—a white woman. *His killers were acquitted.*

You are *not* Trayvon Martin, who was killed in defending his Black innocence. *His killer was also acquitted.*

You are *not* Eric Garner, whose death-rattle, "I Can't Breathe," further initiated an examination of policing against the lives of Black people. This is very different from your own false engagement of the police to service your own purposes. *His killer was also acquitted.*

Maybe you are more like Rachel Dolezal, a white woman who was the protagonist in a national deception centered on race and leadership. Before passing for Black, she too had a history of claiming to be the victim of race-related hate crimes. This was before she committed her *own* race crime and rose to the highest levels as a fake-Black woman in the National Association for the Advancement of Colored People (NAACP).

I am calling you out for using the classic symbols of racism and hatred against Black and gay folks:

the hooded assailant, as in the Ku Klux Klan;

the bleach that seeks to e-race and sanitize identity politics;

and the noose that invokes the historical reality and contemporary legacy of lynching,[6] with *strange fruit* hanging from southern trees, to falsely position yourself as a victim in a theatre of violence. Because of the particularity of your person in a historical pattern of racism, sexism and homophobia, you would be the strange fruit.

You committed a personal assault on truth, justice, peace, families, and on marginalized people living in *real* jeopardy in Trump's America!

You failed to recognize that your hunger for attention and your fake, staged assault promoted as a hate crime actually committed its own crime of hate:

A bias-motivated crime, presumably committed on your Black gay body, was actually committed against the Black men that you accused. It was a crime against the community of police officers and detectives who vigorously investigated the presumed crime against *your* privileged ass at the risk of foregoing the response to real crimes and real victims of hate. This at the same time that other Black brothers are being ritually killed by police officers. But once again—maybe that is your privilege as a celebrity figure now made infamous.

A hate crime was committed against a broader LGBTQ+ community sent into a tailspin when they heard that a rare Black gay public figure in the entertainment industry—one of their homeboys in Chicago—was attacked, only to find out later that you staged the incident as a publicity stunt. But the real hate crime statistics on LGBTQ+ peoples do exist.

A hate crime was committed against the Black men you enlisted to assist you, and against all Black men when you later pointed the finger back at them in a reversal of their fate—our fate—in a reification of history's legacy of Black men always being accused of hate crimes or sexual assaults against the presumed "other," and pitted against one another for the entertainment of others. No laughs then or now, only pain.

A hate crime was committed that reified a social construction of Black men as bestial, violating humanity and performing a hyper-hetero-masculinity that has no room for differences—for the LGBTQ+ community or otherwise—using *a dick-thang masculinity* to control women and gay men.

A hate crime was committed to take advantage of the pain and anger of racism in this country as a self-serving reification of your own privilege. Its goal was to garner attention and popularity either to save your job or increase your salary through public sympathy, creating a broader *empire of doom* for many of us that will last long past your five minutes of fame.

As portions of the United States citizenry, non-citizens living under threat in this country, and people yearning to come to this country are all frightened of our current national leadership—leadership that promotes a politic of hatred and exclusion—for YOU, a doubly marginalized individual in this country, to perpetuate your own self-serving hatred and fear is unconscionable!

Even Donald Trump weighed in that day from the Oval Office, saying that the attack was "horrible" and that it "doesn't get worse."[7] It was not clear to me what he was referencing.

Was it the notion of "black on black crime" that you put into motion—which, from coming him seemed more like a confirmation and critique of *our* Black character, as opposed to concern that it happened to your particular Black ass?

Was his commentary a welcome deflection from the real crimes of police brutalizing and killing everyday unarmed Black men and women as ritual act?

Was he commenting on the attack of a privileged actor on a popular television show by two disenfranchised Nigerian brothers? Maybe this actually served as Trump's evidence for why we need more border controls, more walls, and more immigration bans to keep those criminals, rapists, and colored bodies out of the country?

Or did his words mask chagrin and represent a call to see just how much worse it could actually get, a subtle calling into action of his sleeper cells who want to "Make America Great Again" through a type of racial, ethnic, and gender cleansing? This would not be unlike the intentional use of bleach in your narrative of the attack.

The irony, or not, is that you even claimed that the assailants shouted, "This is MAGA Country!" before they attacked you. M.A.G.A., standing for "Make America Great Again," is a statement that is now its own signifier. It's a clarion call for conservatism, separatism, and hatred: a threat that seeks to turn back time and progress in favor of a more restrictive democracy. The fact that you could even fix your mouth to invoke the phrase is despairing to most Black people. It's different and yet the same as our sick brother Kanye West, who wore the MAGA fucking hat on national television and publicly suggested that African-American slavery was a choice.[8] But that is another rant.

Jussie, I don't deny that evil exists in the world. But your participation in such hate for personal advancement as a publicity stunt is just fucked up! The fact that you were acquitted is little rescue from what you perpetuated. For while you still enjoy the presumption of innocence, these are presumptions and protections under the law that you have exploited to your own advantage.

As a result of your flagrant abuse, I also fear that the police will not respond to members of the LGBTQ+ community—or Black folks— when they/*we* are really attacked and abused, or when they/*we* are really denied free passage and access on the highways and byways of our daily living. But of course that is already happening, isn't it? Thanks for jumping on the bandwagon of disregard for Black—and Gay—Lives that Matter. (*That's sarcasm*).

• • •

As one Black gay man living in America to another;

As one Black gay man living and struggling in a country still rife with racism, sexism, and gender bias to another;

As one Black gay man living in America, where Black males are still suspect and vulnerable to unprovoked violence and accusations of violence;

As one Black gay man living in a country where the content of our character is measured by the performative Blackness and maleness that we present, and LGBTQ+ identities are still *perceived as pathology*;

Your actions that day in January 2019 *promulgated* all those *perceptions* and *presumptions* of our character, and further reduced our *possibility* and *potentiality* to access full *protections* under the law when accused. What a *punk-ass thing to do!

Jussie, here I am taking a simple poetic and performative—yet political—act to talk back to your choices. Such choices will surely impact not just YOUR social perception and marketability, but the mobility of other Black, Black/gay, and particular others walking the streets of Chicago and beyond. It will impact the response to our reports of abuse and attack—even today.

I am in essence not only raising and articulating my voice in performance in/as publication, but to also establish a *template of performative outrage* that exposes, manages, and finesses cultural tensions that must continually be resolved by embodied social subjects. I am engaging in an *autoethnographic rant*: a rapid-fire impassioned social response to actions that one finds egregious. The response is issued in the articulate, controlled, and yet impassioned voice of an experiencing Black gay male body. It exists in a narrative structure with an overtly linear exposure to mapping the offense, effect, and impulse to respond. It exists in relation to a broader cultural context in the way that autoethnography is both particular and plural, both self-experientially related and culturally contextual. It speaks as an act of information, formation, and transformation of self and society. Autoethnography is ultimately about resistance, engagement, and hope—for self and cultural others—as a re-writing of the world.

I am raising my voice to fight back with my words and writing; and using the particularity of my voice as another to resist and to say again, "Fuck you!"

> This is not *just* using the phrase, "Fuck you!" for shock value, or to use the perceived profane or uncouth social construction that some might think belies my intelligence or my position.

> I use the phrase as an "activist affect"[9]: a performance of protest and resistance with a productive emotionality directed against not just your abuse of the judicial system, or the manipulation of the media, or even your accusation against the two Nigerian brothers. I use it as an exclamation of your personal assault against me as another Black gay man who must now live in a world that has been further harmed by your selfish action. Yes, I take your actions personally.

> I use the phrase, "Fuck you!" as a potent explication of disdain, as a reverse adjectival prepositional phrase in which the adjective resists being subordinated and stands before the subject pronoun: you.

> I use it as a method of both invoking and inciting outrage in a very visceral way that undergirds protest that leads to response.

> I use "Fuck you!" as a performative phrase that does something in the world and functions as a social action, as did you, when you claimed that your assailants shouted, "This is MAGA country." In the moment of the presumed attack, the utterance both accredited and acted out its intention as a politic of doing as a politic of hatred, an action of erasure that reverses the hands of time back to when Africans and Black Americans-to-be were enslaved and Jim Crow'ed.

And yes, I use this coarse phrase as an intensifier, as a guttural outcry from your sucker punch to my solar plexus. Your actions fueled an already problematic climate of hatred and exclusion—one which literally takes my breath away. "I CAN'T BREATHE, BROTHER!"

I know the impact of these words.

I am a Black Brotha with a PhD, a *Brotha Docta*.[10]

I have other words.

But "Fuck You!" is the phrase that best expresses the immediacy of my felt response, which lingers with me when I think of you. The words invoke a positionality against your ill repute. For these are the words, probably dismissive in nature, that you also figuratively uttered in the moment of plotting your scheme against social propriety. So I also use my words with exacting precision and intentionality to critique your choices.

If you haven't noticed: This is not a fan letter. In fact, it is a call for a boycott of your *empire* and the viability of your ever being a public figure or role model, in any mode or medium, despite your ongoing self-promotion. Harsh? Maybe.

So, it is important for me to acknowledge that all *Black Lives Matter*, including yours.

Ever mindful of our futures, and the continued struggles ahead,

ABlackGayManLivingandStrugglinginAmerica.

Author's Note

A variation of this piece was produced and performed at the May 2019 International Congress of Qualitative Inquiry at the University of Illinois, Urbana-Champagne on a panel organized by Christopher Poulus entitled, *Autoethnography, Resistance, Engagement, Hope.*

Notes

1   See Chicago Police Department Chief Superintendent Eddie T. Johnson's (February 21, 2019) news conference on the case (https://www.youtube.com/watch?v=zUSnegQd-RQ; https://www.chicagotribune.com/news/local/breaking/ct-met-cb-jussie-smollett-20190215-story.html).

2   Black Lives Matter: All italicized quotes are taken from the article by Carissimo and McNamara (2020).

3   Here, I riff on both: Langston Hughes' "dream deferred" poem (Hughes, n.d.) and Martin Luther King Jr.'s "I Have a Dream" speech (King, 1963).

4   For a timeline of the case, see Arnold (2019).

5   Jussie Smollett played a Black gay character on the television show *Empire*. I make several references—including *empire, empire of terror,* and *empire of doom*—without critiquing the show proper (see Empire (2015 TV series), n.d.).

6   See Fuoss (1999).

7   See Earle (2019).

8   See Snapes (2019) and BBC News (2018).

9   See Harris and Holman (2018).

10 See Jones (1997).

Hanging Chads?

Bryant Keith Alexander

Dear Mary,

The signifiers of "attached" and "still hanging" make me think of the phrase "hanging chads," but only in a sardonic kind of way. Or maybe that is a sarcastic way, or maybe that is just a scandalous kind of way. I have only heard those two words in relation to the debacle of the 2000 United States presidential election. It referred to a flaw in the Votomatic-style, punched-card ballots. Incomplete punched holes resulted in partially punched "chads"—meaning one or more corners were still attached. The chads were left hanging and thus counted as unverifiable Democratic Party votes for then-Vice President Al Gore. This lead to the Republican governor of Texas, George W. Bush, eventually winning by a narrow margin.

Scandalous because before then, I had never heard of a "hanging Chad." I had only heard of a hanging Toby, or a hanging Old George, or a hanging young George, an Otis "Titi" or a Robert Fuller; a Dominique; maybe a Rayshard, a Sandra, a Breonna. An endless list of Black bodies, left hanging or slain, that never seemed to cause so much disturbance relative to the insurance and execution of the democratic process, as a hanging chad.

Bryant

© BRYANT KEITH ALEXANDER, 2021 | DOI: 10.1163/9789004464858_018

PART 2

Bodies on the Line

⁚

Attached?

Mary E. Weems

CBS News Report. Southfield, Georgia. Black Woman found attached to
a tree

When you dead
you can hear and smell everything
the still air, slight scent of old peaches and magnolias
sound of the click made thousands of miles away to find
the CBS news report about where I was found
unknown and unidentified

I'd stopped at Walmart after a long day at work
needed some Almond milk and pork rinds, grabbed
a six-pack of soda last minute, just in case we'd run out at home

While I was standing in line, I noticed three white men wearing
MAGA Hats, not-looking at me the way white folks do when they
pretending like they haven't attached their gaze to you like gorilla glue.

Made me nervous, but I thought *Walmart's got cameras everywhere,*
plus I been working out, so if I need to run, I can.

Cashier handed me my Debit card, noted I was almost down to my last ten
dollars with this purchase, I'd been through her line a thousand times
so didn't mind, thanked her, looked around, no MAGA hats.
Started breathing. Relieved I step outside to walk to my car.

I almost made it.

Scanned the close-to-dark lot before I opened the front door, put my purse
on the driver's seat, turned to open the back and three MAGA hats popped up
like the three stooges at the beginning of a movie.
One put his hand over my mouth, the other grabbed me around the waist,
the third snatched my feet off the ground.

© MARY E. WEEMS, 2021 | DOI: 10.1163/9789004464858_019

I tried to fight, but they had me trapped like a hog about to be slaughtered.

I could smell the almost-summer breeze, it felt warm and welcoming
like I was getting ready to sit down in my yard for some sweet tea.

Instead they took me to the way-in-the-back east end of the lot
where a stand of trees lined the fence

put a knotted rope around my neck, called me a nigger bitch,
tied the other end to a thick branch
and dropped me.

Dead people can't tell time, but it felt like a while before two
white police officers approached with their guns drawn
like I was in front of them, standing on ground, alive and dangerous.
I hear them talking:

*Well I'll be damned Jim, not another one. You're over me, what'll we report
on this one?*

*Shit, I don't know Hunter. With all this shit already going on
down here, we can't say 'lynched,' hell we can't even say 'rope.'*

You got that right. So, what'll we say. Whatever it is. I'm with you.

(Jim, takes his note pad out of his pocket and begins to write)

Okay, how about this:
*Unidentified Black female found at 8:03 p.m. in the east end of the Southfield
Walmart. She appears to be dead and is attached to a tree. What you think,
Hunter?*

*Sounds okey, dokey to me sir. Let's call the body bag people and get the hell outta
here, time for dinner.*

CHAPTER 12

Still Hanging?

Bryant Keith Alexander

FIGURE 9   Victims of lynch mob hanging from tree. (Source: Getty Images)

It is the year 2020 and Black people are still being hanged.
It is the year 2020 and Black bodies of differing ages and genders are being hanged.
It is the year 2020 and Black bodies are still found hanging:

> a black 17-year-old hanged outside an elementary school in Houston.

© BRYANT KEITH ALEXANDER, 2021 | DOI: 10.1163/9789004464858_020

a Hispanic man hanged outside a store in the community of Shady Acres, Houston.

the body of Otis "Titi" Gulley, 31, a homeless black man who identified as a woman, hanging from a tree in Rocky Butte Park, according to the Portland Mercury.

Malcolm Harsch, 38, was found in Victorville on May 31.

Robert Fuller, 24, was found 53 miles away, hanged on June 10 at a park near Palmdale City Hall.

New York borough of Manhattan, 27-year-old Dominique Alexander was found hanging from a tree at Fort Tryon Park on June 9.

"Woman's body found hanging from tree outside Walmart in Georgia."[1]

It is the year 2020 and Black bodies are found hanging and the investigative reports suggest suicide?

I want to know: I want to know just how many African people were killed by hanging before kidnapped to these United States of America (much less committed suicide by hanging)?

I want to know how many Black people in the history of this country have committed suicide, and then how many committed suicide by hanging?

I want to know how many Black people with knowledge of the history of slavery, Jim Crow, and the white resistance to the emancipation of slaves in these United States of America—kill themselves by hanging? *That does not seem plausible.*[2]

I want to know how many Black people—with a historical, psychic/blood/ body memory of the history of slavery and racism in this country choose suicide by the ancient weapon and threat of Massa to kill and punish Black resistance and to make public spectacle and the race-based devaluation of human life as town square events or picnics; as an object lesson to other would-be uppity-resistant-freedom seekers of African descent—would choose hanging as the operative method to end their personal suffering in the year 2020?

I wonder if their names and stories will be placed at the *lynching memorial* in the literal place of historicizing this national atrocity, or just emblazoned in our hearts and seared in our memory; their living and how they died as a testimony to Black struggle.[3]

FIGURE 10   Britain attacks military murder (noose). (Source: Getty Images)

These current-day lynching and hanging are happening in a time with an unprecedented Black Lives Matters Movement and activism around the country. The resurgent hangings and the lynching of Black folks comes as backlash,

as a white reminder of history;

as a white reminder of the power structures of this country under the presidency of Donald J. Trump, and his clarion call to "Make America Great Again";

as an act of retribution: with whites losing their territorial imperative— losing ground against their assumed white superiority and being made accountable—they are now openly wearing their red MAGA hats, not their white hoods, and just snatching and hanging Black folks.

and this attacking on some of the most vulnerable or momentarily isolated Black folks, and hanging them in public spaces, and practiced places, is a desperate continued practice of power;

as a message and warning—like in some cases just the terrorizing symbol of nooses anonymously left in locations around the country in recent days.

It is the Year 2020 and Black People Are Still Being Hanged

Let's think about that.

Let's talk about that.

Still.

Author's Note

This piece was inspired by the headlines of these modern-day hangings, with riffs on the article: Lee, A. (2020, June 24.) 5 people of color have died in recent string of hangings across country. *The Atlanta Journal-Constitution.* https://www.ajc.com/news/people-color-have-died-recent-string-hangings-across-country/dwYcL9kK7vRYn4ZqwofigL/

Notes

1   See CBS News (2018).
2   See Vives (2020).
3   See Young (2010).

A Crack in My Heart

Bryant Keith Alexander

Dear Mary,

I remember writing to you:

> So, this morning I found myself reading your play, 'Crack the door for some Air.' I read it not only on June 12th as a remembrance of the Orlando tragedy, and our response to it. But I read it this morning as the news headlines are rife with stories of civil unrest and social activism and riots and sheer outrage over the continued murdering of unarmed Black people at the hands of police in America.
>
> In reading your play my breath was taken away—both by the banality of everyday living and the traumas of survival that challenge our faith and perseverance, and the power of Black love. But also, the scary subtlety of factors that we seemingly have no control over. For me, the title, 'Crack the door for some Air,' juxtaposed two aspects of daily living that stand in stark relief: the mostly Black and Southern colloquialism of asking someone to 'put a crack in the door or the window' for air circulation, and the now pained anthem of our lives, 'I Can't Breathe.' The first makes me smile as a Black Southerner now academic. The second makes me cry from the crack in my heart. I am grateful for your particular focus of a full-length drama in response to the killing of innocent Black women by police.
>
> I am asking the question, 'Are the lives of Black women worth less than the lives of Black men?' This play forces use to think and feel into the question, and into the inequities of silence even in despair. I am with you sister.

The memory of reading the play for the first time is still fresh in my mind.
Your brother,

Bryant

© BRYANT KEITH ALEXANDER, 2021 | DOI: 10.1163/9789004464858_021

Crack the Door for Some Air

Mary E. Weems

This play was created in protest of the murder of Atatiana Jefferson by police, and the deaths of all other Black women killed by police, including Sandra Bland, who was found hanging by a garbage bag in her jail cell. While the heart of the play is based on fact—a Black woman shot by police through the window while playing video games with her nephew in her mother's house—the balance is imagined by the playwright.

Characters:

Tamara:	28-year-old Black woman; middle-class background.
Mumia:	10–15-year-old Black male; Tamara's nephew.
Jeff:	29-year-old Black male; Tamera's long-time best friend and fiancé.
Mama/	
Ms. Johnson:	50s to early 60s Black woman; Tamara's mother. Also, Voiceover.
Kayla:	10- to 15-year-old Black female; Mumia's girlfriend.
B-Roll:	50s Black male; Kayla's uncle. One of the leaders of the D-Dogs gang.
Brother:	50s, Black male; first member of HABO.
*Sylvester:	Black male neighbor who calls non-emergency police number (Voiceover only)

Act I, Scene I:

(*Setting: Tamara's apartment. She's walking in the front door after work, talking on her cell phone, getting some bad news about her mother, who can be seen talking on her cell phone in her home as they talk.*)

Tamara:	But that's not what we're talking about right now, mama.
Mama:	Did you just raise your voice to me, Tamara Edwina Johnson?
Tamara:	No, no of course not mama, I'm just worried.
Mama:	I know you are Tee-Tee, but I keep trying to tell you, God got this.
Tamara:	Yeah, but like that old white actor once said, "God answers all prayers but sometimes the answer is, No."

© MARY E. WEEMS, 2021 | DOI: 10.1163/9789004464858_022

Mama: No, you're not quoting Kirk Douglas, girl stop.

Tamara: I told you I'm upset, I don't even know where that came from... Just please know that all your arguments for why I can't use some of this paid time off I've accumulated and stay with you till you get better are not going to work. I'm coming to see about you asap.

(*Silence*)

Tamara: Mama?

Mama: Okay, Tee-Tee, call me tomorrow.

Tamara: I will.

Mama: Love you.

Tamara: Love you more, bye-bye.

(*Tamara and her mother hang up. Tamara takes off her sweater, drops her keys in the dish in the hallway, and dials her boss as lights fade out.*)

Tamara: Hello, Mr. Pendleton. I need to speak with you as soon as possible. (*Listens*) My mother's ill and I need to move in with her for a while. (*Listens.*) Tomorrow evening at 6:30 p.m., your office. See you then, thanks.

End of Scene

Act I, Scene II:

(*Later that same evening, Jeff drops by for a visit. They embrace.*)

Jeff: How's your day been Tee?

Tamara: I'll tell you in a minute; first, how did things go at HABO today?

Jeff: I keep asking you not to keep reducing Help-A-Brother-Out to an acronym. I know we live in the age of language shorthand, POTUS, GMA, SMH etc. but, I'm trying to get the mission and the message handled in four words.

Tamara: Sorry, baby. Between the job, spending all day talking to mutual fund clients, and talking to family about mama, I'm trying to use as few words as possible right about now. How's Help-A-Brother-Out going?

Jeff: Keeping me stressed out, trying to get the young men in our family to listen more and rap about their lives a little less, but it's a

	joyful stress because I know even when I think they're not paying attention, they never forget I care.
Tamara:	I know that's right. Mama likes to say that you can't teach anyone anything unless you first, show them you care. By the way, it's been three years, how's the word 'brother' catching on?
Jeff:	I've been waiting for you to ask that question. I recall your argument for 'brother' being a term from the '60s and '70s.
Tamara:	It was.
Jeff:	Right, but as I said back then, the word needs to come back and the fact is, not one of the young and not-so-young men who are part of us, have had a problem with it. Did I ever tell you where I got the name from?
Tamara:	I think you started to one day but we got sidetracked. Tell me.
Jeff:	I was on my way into Pay-a-Lot about four years ago, it was a hot-as-hell August morning, and I saw this what looked like to me able-bodied Black man standing by the entrance. As I got closer, I could tell something was wrong, but as if embarrassed to beg, he waited until I turned to walk inside before I heard him say "Can you help a brother out?"
Tamara:	Damn. What did you do?
Jeff:	I went in the in-door and walked right back out of the exit door, looked him in the eye, put 20 dollars in his hand along with my business card and asked him to be in touch if I could help him. I won't share his name, but he was one of the first ten men between 18 and 50 to join us. As you know, I'd been talking about doing something to help brothers since we were in high school. That was what made me get my ass in gear.
Tamara:	And every time I see the look on your face when you talk about it, I'm reminded of why I love you.
Jeff:	I don't know about all that, now. What's all the butter for this evening? What do you want?
Tamara:	I don't want anything. Do I have to want something to tell you how I feel about you?
Jeff:	Nope, but it's not what you're saying, it's how. What's up?
Tamara:	It's mama.
Jeff:	What's going on? Tell me.
Tamara:	Her cancer's back.
Jeff:	Damn, again? I'm so sorry Tee.

(*He reaches out to embrace her.*)

Tamara:	Me too. Fourth time, same breast.
Jeff:	I remember. Is she still?
Tamara:	Smoking Kool's? Hell, yes. She's stopped smoking when she talks to me on the phone because she knows how much I hate to hear her huffing and puffing, but she's always honest about having absolutely no interest in quitting.
Jeff:	She still doesn't believe cigarettes cause cancer, does she?
Tamara:	No. At least after three times in the same breast, Dr. Lang's finally been able to convince her to have a mastectomy.
Jeff:	Thank God for that, baby. What can I do to help?
Tamara:	Just keep doing what you always have baby, you're so sensitive to what I need on a daily, even when I'm in denial.
Jeff:	I try my best Tee. One of the things I love about you is that I don't have to 'wonder' what's on your mind, you tell me straight up and that helps me stay in tune.
Tamara:	Right now, the only thing on my mind is mama. Mama going through all of this cancer treatment shit again, mama losing one of the breasts she fed me with when I was a baby, mama continuing to smoke in denial when I 'know' it's going to kill her eventually if she doesn't stop.

(*Jeff puts his arm around her and they sit side-by-side heads touching for a few moments.*)

Jeff:	Tee, I understand. How can you not worry, but please take a minute to remind yourself who's in control, not me, not you, not your mama, even though she could choose to stop smoking.
Tamara:	I know...the Creator.
Jeff:	Yes. God's running this and all we can do is our best to love the people we love, do what we can when they need support. If either of us could run the world, your mama wouldn't be sick, Black men wouldn't be walking around with metaphorical targets on their backs, and you and me...
Tamara:	You and me what?
Jeff:	Never mind. I'll tell you later. Right now, let's figure out what I need to do to get you ready to get out of here asap.
Tamara:	Then why did you start a sentence you're not ready to finish?
Jeff:	Like I said, later Tee. I promise, I won't forget. Let's get your business straight first.

(Tamara's cell phone rings as he's leaving.)

Tamara: Hello? Oh, hi Mama, how are you doing?

(Lights fade to black.)

End of Scene

Act I, Scene III:

(Two weeks later. Moving day. Tamara's packing and Jeff comes by to pick up a load for storage. The door's cracked, and Jeff enters without knocking.)

Tamara:	Hey, baby.
Jeff:	Tee! How many times have I told you to stop leaving this door cracked?
Tamara:	I know. I just opened it for a few minutes to let some fresh air in.
Jeff:	I know why you do it. A bad habit you picked up from your mother when you were growing up.
Tamara:	Correction, not my mother, my grandmother, mama's mother. If you know it's a habit, why do you keep checking me about it?
Jeff:	Because it was a bad idea twenty years ago, and it's a bad idea now. Please baby.
Tamara:	Alright, I'll do my best, can't promise because I do it almost without thinking, but I'll try.
Jeff:	You still have that heart shaped box your mama gave you when you were five years-old?
Tamara:	Yep...I call it my Care Box. It has things that remind me of good days in my life.
Jeff:	I didn't know that. You showed me the box when we were in elementary school, but that was to tell me that at one time it was filled with your mama's homemade chocolate cupcakes, when she gave it to you for your birthday. What's in it?
Tamara:	None of your business.
Jeff:	Come on now, you don't have to show me everything. Anything in there about us?

(Tamara opens the box, takes out an old paper popcorn bag, her Freshman prom program, and a condom, and lays them out on the floor.)

Tamara:	Remember the first time you took me on an unofficial date? I never told you this, but after you drew me that Valentine Card in the 5th grade, I came home and told mama I liked you, and she told me I was too young to like anything other than school, cartoons, riding my bike, and playing outside.
Jeff:	She did? Not surprised. She's forgotten more than two of us know about how relationships work and probably knew our hormones would be kicking in soon.
Tamara:	In the 5th grade?
Jeff:	I can't speak for you Tee, but I'm certain I was feeling something I shouldn't have when I drew you that Valentine and when you gave me that smile and I looked in those deep-dark brown eyes of yours—I was hooked.
Tamara:	Anyway, this popcorn bag is the first bag you ever bought me at the old Liberty theater. I was so happy, I kept the bag and used to open it and smell the butter, to take me back to that day.
Jeff:	You remember the name of the movie?
Tamara:	Yep. Independence Day with Will Smith!
Jeff:	Still one of my favorites.

(*Tamara picks up the program.*)

Tamara:	I was always so proud to be dating an older boy.
Jeff:	I was only a year ahead of you.
Tamara:	Yes, but when you're in the 10th grade, dating an 11th grader, that's huge. I fell out with a lot of my so-called girlfriends who had crushes on you. Especially, Tasty.
Jeff:	Tasty? Oh, you mean Jasmine.
Tamara:	You know who I mean.
Jeff:	Tee, now that's mean. I never called her that and I think she got a bad rap for one mistake.
Tamara:	No, you're right you didn't. We girls named her that because she was always licking her lips when a boy we liked walked by. What bad mistake?
Jeff:	Uh, never mind. If you haven't known about it all these years, far be it from me to add to the story...We had a good time that night, didn't we?
Tamara:	Yes, we did!

(*She gets up and begins ballroom-ing around the room. Jeff joins her for a moment or two.*)

Jeff: I'll never forget that sky blue lacy dress...it was the first time I'd
            ever seen you in lipstick and heels and ooooo whee! You looked
            good enough to—
Tamara: Which brings me to this condom.
Jeff: Right. The condom 'you' had in your evening bag.
Tamara: We'd just had health class the week before and you know our
            Health teacher Ms. Hamilton didn't hold back when it came to
            sex.
Jeff: How well I remember, if I could turn red, I'd have blushed my way
            through every one of her classes back then.
Tamara: That day she gave us all condoms, the boys so they'd remember
            to use one if they got lucky, and the girls in case we decided to let
            them.
Jeff: Damn. I wish I'd known. Hell, back then I thought about having
            sex all the time, but at sixteen I was still a virgin, respected you
            a lot, and regardless of what I was thinking, I never would have
            come on to you in the 10th grade, you were only fifteen.
Tamara: Humph! Yes, I know what the law says about that, and I appreci-
            ate the respect, but I had similar feelings about you, most of my
            girlfriends had been having sex for months and had you tried,
            you probably would have gotten lucky.

(She takes one more thing from the box. Jeff's dad's obituary.)

Jeff: You kept this? Why?
Tamara: Because I loved your daddy too...I'll never forget the look on your
            face, when all of his fellow officers showed up at Ebeneezer Bap-
            tist to give your dad the official police sendoff he deserved. All
            those men in dress blues, the white gloves, his pastor's face as he
            watched.
Jeff: Tee...It's been five years, I still can't talk about it. Killed on a
            bullshit humble. Doesn't even help that the man who shot him
            during that traffic stop will never see the light of day as long as he
            lives either. Dad's still dead.
Tamara: I know baby, you don't have to. Just wanted you to know, I haven't
            forgotten. I'll keep this in my Care Box always.

(He comes to put his head on her shoulder for a moment. Regains his composure.)

(Tamara puts the items back in her Care Box.)

Tamara:	I'm taking this with me, but there's a few boxes over in the corner you can take, while I finish packing.
Jeff:	What about the furniture?
Tamara:	I'm leaving the couch, dining room table and chairs, end tables, lamps all the big stuff here.
Jeff:	Aren't you concerned about it being damaged?
Tamara:	Nope. This is why I'm working with Jess. You know she has her own property management business.
Jeff:	That's right, I'd forgotten about her. It's been so long. Good point.
Tamara:	Thanks to Jess, I know Ms. Ellie Johnson will be a good tenant and if she's not, my sublease has me covered for all possibilities, plus she has to have renter's insurance before she moves in.
Jeff:	Excellent. My science teacher used to say expect the best, but prepare for the worst. Sounds like Jess has helped you cover all bases.
Tamara:	Definitely. Now, help me out by getting those boxes out of here for me so I can get back to work.
Jeff:	Your wish is my command.
Tamara:	Yeah, right. See you later tonight, baby.
Jeff:	Not if I see you first.

(*Jeff exits laughing, as Tamara's cell phone rings.*)

Tamara:	Hello? Hi mama, how are you doing?
Mama (VO):	I'm doing good, Tee-Tee. You finished packing yet?
Tamara:	Packing as we speak. I should be finished by tomorrow, then I'll have two days to take care of other stuff like changing my mailing address to your house and getting the place clean before Ms. Bailey moves in at the end of the month.
Mama:	Sounds like a plan. Looking forward to seeing you Sunday night daughter...It's been too long since you've been here. I miss you.
Tamara:	Miss you too, mama. Wish the circumstances were better, but we'll make the most of our time.
Mama:	You got that right. Speaking of time, I've made another decision about my health.
Tamara:	What!?
Mama:	Don't get upset, before I even tell you.
Tamara:	Okay, then what?
Mama:	I've thought it over, done my research, even talked to some women my doctor recommended who've already been through it.

Tamara:	Mama, please cut to the end. Been through what?
Mama:	I've decided to have a double mastectomy.
Tamara:	(*Beat*) Why? Did they suddenly find cancer in your other breast?
Mama:	No, at least not yet.
Tamara:	What do you mean?
Mama:	I mean, the chances of someone like me, who's had breast cancer four times getting it in the other breast are high.
Tamara:	Meaning?
Mama:	I don't remember the exact percentage, but it was high enough I decided not to take the chance on leaving it.
Tamara:	Are you sure? What did the women you talked to say?
Mama:	It was interesting. Each of the three women had a different reason for deciding on a double.
Tamara:	Okay, even though at this point, part of me doesn't give a shit what their reasons were, humor me.
Mama:	First woman I called was Dolly. She's 72 and was 68 when she had her double. Told me her breasts had always felt like foreign objects to her, and for that reason, even though she didn't smoke, she wasn't surprised when she got cancer in her right breast.
Tamara:	Same breast as yours.
Mama:	Right. When I asked her why her breasts felt like they didn't belong on her body, she said she didn't exactly know, but they had and she was looking forward to being flat chested. Wasn't worried about the scars at this stage of her life and had no plans for breast reconstruction.
Tamara:	Damn...God bless her. I can't imagine, but what's important is what works for her. What about the other two?
Mama:	Rhonda was only 32 when she had her double. Seems breast cancer runs in her family. Her mother had it, her grandmother had it and both of her older sisters. For her it was a practical decision. Before she caught cancer the first time, she talked it over with her husband Jack and they agreed. Had her double, breast reconstruction and was doing fine last time we talked.
Tamara:	Wow. And I think we have problems. Breasts removed because she more than likely will catch it—damn. What about the third woman?
Mama:	Laura was the only Black woman he hooked me up with. For her, it was about economics. She was 60, about to lose her job and excellent health insurance when she found out, and told the doctor rather than wish in one hand and spit in the other

'hoping' she'd be okay in the future, cut them both off now. That way, she'll have one less thing to worry about. Last time we talked she'd been unemployed two years—no prospects.

Tamara: Sounds like age discrimination is alive and well.

Mama: And like race discrimination, almost impossible to prove. I keep her in my prayers.

Tamara: Oh snap, look at the time. Mama I have to get off this phone. Need to finish packing. Jeff will be back later to pick up another load and I want to be almost done with the stuff I'm putting into storage.

Mama: Okay, Tee-Tee. Talk to you later. Love you.

Tamara: Love you more, Mama. Bye-bye.

End of Scene

Act I, Scene IV:

(*Later that same night at Tamara's house. Jeff rings the doorbell, then knocks immediately as if anxious to get in. He's dressed in a tux and carrying a heart-shaped box and a single red rose.*)

Tamara: Jeff, have you lost what's left of your mind? Rose, box of choco-lates? How are you going to haul boxes in a tux?

(*Jeff walks slowly towards her, places the rose in her cleavage, the heart-shaped box in her hand, grabs her other hand, guides her to the middle of the packing mess, drops on one knee.*)

Tamara: Hey, what? Wait a minute, wait a minute, baby, what are you doing? I'm on my way—

Jeff: Tee-Tee, stop!

(*Tamara falls silent.*)

Jeff: My dad always told me, that I'd know when I met the woman I'll be with the rest of my life. He said if you marry your best friend, you'll never be lonely.

Tamara: Baby, stop, I—

Jeff: I can't stop now, Tee, I'm on one knee and it's my bad one, so please let me finish.

(*Tamara gets on her knees in front of him.*)

Jeff: I think of you almost all the time. I'll be in the middle of a hard
             day at the foundation, meeting yet another rich person, and I'll
             think of something you said the day before and it'll make me
             laugh. Every time I sit at your table, your cooking tastes like more,
             your lips are what I want to be kissing just before I die.

(*He puts the heart-shaped box in her left hand.*)

Jeff: Tamara Edwina Johnson, will you complete me by agreeing to
             take my hand in marriage?

(*Tamara takes a few moments to look him deep in the eyes before she responds.*)

Tamara: Yes, yes, I will Jeff. I'd be honored to be your wife, I promise I'll
             love you, be by your side through whatever comes, hold your
             hand through the worst and best times for the rest of my life.

(*She drops the box, they embrace each other.*)

Jeff: Open the box Tee.

(*Tamara opens the box, and instead of candy it's another box. She opens it and
inside is a beautiful diamond engagement ring.*)

Tamara: Oh my God Jeff, you can't afford this! It's beautiful.
Jeff: Last thing on my mind right now is what I can't afford, darling.
             Glad you love it, let's see how it looks.

(*He kisses her left hand, slides the ring on the third finger.*)

Tamara: Perfect fit. I didn't even know you knew my ring size.
Jeff: That's what future mother-in-laws are for.
Tamara: You mean, mama knew?
Jeff: As of yesterday, yes. I swore her to secrecy.
Tamara: Secrecy? I didn't know mama even knew how to spell 'secrecy,'
             she can't keep a doctor's appointment secret.
Jeff: Just goes to show, even she can keep a secret when she wants to.

Tamara: Enough about mama, let's go upstairs. I have something to show you about love and it's going to take a while.

(*They kiss deeply as stage darkens to black.*)

End of Act I

Act II, Scene I

(*Setting: Tamara's mother's house. It's night time and a tired Tamara knocks on her mama's door, she has a suitcase in each hand.*)

Mama: Tee-Tee! It's about time. Come here and give your mama a hug, girl, it's been too long.

(*Tamara drops the suitcases and embraces her mama.*)

Tamara: Hey, mama-mia, it's been a long day. So glad to finally be here.
Mama: Me too. Let's get you settled in and I'll fix you something to eat.
Tamara: Okay, but I'm not hungry right now, mama.
Mama: Not even for dessert? I made your favorite, my homemade peach cobbler and I have some French vanilla ice cream to top it off.
Tamara: In that case, let me drop this stuff and take a shower. I'll be back down so we can talk while I enjoy this little bit of heaven you baked.
Mama: Sounds like a plan, Tee-Tee, I'll get it ready.

(*Mama exits to the kitchen to begin preparing dessert and setting it on the kitchen table with two glasses of milk, as Tamara goes to the downstairs spare bedroom. Mumia enters through the front door.*)

Mumia: Granny, where are you? I see Auntie's car, where is she?
Mama: Hey, Mummy.

(*Mama checks her watch.*)

Mama: You just made curfew young man, where you been?

(*Mumia tries to give her a hug, but she stops him.*)

Mama:	Uh-uh, don't try to hug your way into another subject, I said where have you been?
Mumia:	At the library, Granny, isn't that where I told you I was going when I stopped at home after school today?
Mama:	Yes, and you tell me all kinds of stuff, Mummy. I keep telling you I used to be 15 too.
Mumia:	I know Granny not trying to be shady.
Mama:	Shady, you trying to be a tree? Not only shoot me some b.s., but hide the sun from me while you're doing it?
Mumia:	Nope, not at all. I know 'you' know the library closed at 9, I know 'you' know exactly how much time it takes me to get home from there because you told me when you upped my curfew from 7:30 to 9 when I turned 15.
Mama:	Yes, okay, so you know I know, now where were you really because you've never, ever came home from the library late, ever.
Mumia:	Okay, okay, I was at the library but I did leave something out.
Mama:	Which was?
Mumia:	I was talking to a girl the whole time except the first half hour it took Ms. Robinson to help me find the books I needed for this report.
Mama:	Oh, so you met a girl? What about Lisa? She was your forever girlfriend just last week, right?
Mumia:	Come on, Gran you know Lisa and me have been friends since we were in first grade, why do you keep insisting she's my girlfriend?
Mama:	Because I love everything about that girl, she's smart, her mother and father are good people and she's crazy about you.
Mumia:	Since when?
Mama:	Since ever since I've been knowing her, Mummy. It's like the two of you are in a different relationship, you think she's your friend and she's been making wedding plans since the 4th grade.
Mumia:	If that's the case, then why are you just telling me about it?
Mama:	Mummy, if you don't get your behind out of my face with this mess. Your head is hard as titanium, I've been telling you the same thing for years. Your problem is, you don't want to hear it. You've written your own story about the two of you, and you just keep adding sentences that say what you want them to say instead of doing the one thing that will make everything perfectly clear.
Mumia:	Gran, I'm only 15, I don't want to be clear right now. I want to feel like I felt when I was with that girl, I just met...Did I tell you she's already 16, goes to Foremost—

Mama:	Foremost? That's that ritzy private school. Wow, what else?
Mumia:	And she makes me feel different, different in ways I can't talk to you about.
Mama:	Ohhhhh, so it's like that?
Mumia:	Yep, it's like that. I was so excited I don't even know her name. When I saw her seated at the table with her head bent over a book, I walked up, introduced myself and we started talking like we've been knowing each other a long time.

(*Tamara enters.*)

| Tamara: | Mummy! My God, come here, young man. |
| Mumia: | Auntie! |

(*They embrace for several seconds.*)

Tamara:	Wait a minute, step back. Let me look at you. Mummy, when I saw you last year, I could still pop you on the top of that big head of yours, now you got the nerve to be tall enough to look me in the eye. You see this, mama?
Mama:	Sure do, but he's been taller than me since he was 12, so I guess I don't notice it as much since I see him every day.
Mumia:	Come on now, auntie, have I changed that much?
Tamara:	Let's see. You remember the dap you taught me last year?
Mumia:	Yep.

(*They take time to do a complex hand maneuver, Tamara messes up the last move and they both laugh.*)

Mama:	Alright, you two. Let's go in the kitchen so I can make up another bowl of pie and ice cream for Mummy. We can talk while we eat.
Mumia:	What kind Granny?
Tamara:	Peach cobbler, what else? After all, I'm the one that's come to visit. What did you think it was, your favorite?
Mumia:	Yep. French apple. One top crust, loaded with apples and covered with evaporated milk, just like my mother used to make.

(*Tamara and mama exchange a look Mumia doesn't see. They sit down around the table and begin enjoying their desserts and talking.*)

Tamara:	Hmmmm, mmm. Just like always mama, not-too-sweet, warm and melt in your mouth.
Mama:	Glad you're enjoying it, Tee-Tee. Will make it whenever you want it while you're here.
Tamara:	Thanks, mama. Mummy, tell me everything. What's been going on?
Mumia:	Auntie, it's almost 10 o'clock at night, I can't possibly go over a whole year of stuff in the ten minutes I have to finish this pie.
Mama:	You're right about that, grandson. How about you give your auntie the main parts now and fill in the blanks when you see her tomorrow after school?
Tamara:	That will work, nephew. What's been up with you?
Mumia:	A lot. They changed the name of our school from Thomas Jefferson to Langston Hughes High for one thing.
Tamara:	They did? Lord have mercy. Mama, we know how long folks in this neighborhood have been fighting to make that happen.
Mama:	Yes, we do Tee-Tee. Since way back when you were a little girl.
Tamara:	What happened? What was the straw that finally killed that camel a.k.a. white folks' tradition around here?
Mama:	You know I finally got off the school name committee after too many years, two years ago.
Tamara:	Yes, I remember you told me.
Mama:	And after several of us older folks stepped down, we finally figured out what the missing ingredient was.
Mumia:	She's talking about us, auntie. After Granny stepped down and some others, Jake, a white student in the 11th grade was asked to do some research in history class and decided to find out more about his father's hero.
Tamara:	Thomas Jefferson?
Mumia:	Yep, exactly. Once he found out what a slave owning, Indian killing, raping scoundrel he was—
Tamara:	Okay, I understand but what about all of the good things he did?
Mumia:	Good point. Like all of us, Jake had already heard of the good stuff his first semester here. His problem was it was a half-assed—
Mama:	Watch your mouth young man.
Mumia:	Ooops, sorry Granny, I meant we were all taught only part of his story. When Jake found out, he contacted everybody on Instagram. Posted a picture of himself with tears running down his eyes with a note that said "Thomas Jefferson is not a hero. Time to change our name."

Tamara: Damn, and just like that it happened?

Mama: Of course not, Tee-Tee, you know better than that. Let Mummy finish.

Mumia: Turns out Jake's dad used to be a union organizer. When Jake told him everything he'd learned and after his father doublechecked his evidence, he decided to help his son and formed a committee of outraged students and parents from all grade levels. I even convinced Granny to come back and help us, didn't I?

Mama: Aw, well, I didn't do much. Baked some things, called some folks. Did a one old-woman sit in, in front of the principal's office.

Mumia: Auntie, I'll never forget that day, Granny didn't even tell anyone she was going to do it. We'd just met with the principal for the umpteenth time, he'd said *No* again, and we were getting frustrated. Jake's dad recommended we meet the following Sunday after the football game and before dinner, but that next Monday—

Mama: The head janitor is a friend of mine. I got him to let me in at 7:15 a.m. before school started. I dressed up like a slave and put a sign on my back that said "My name is not Sally Hemming, but Thomas Jefferson owned me too," and when the principal arrived at 8 o'clock, he saw me sitting on the floor in front of his office with a white bandana on my head and tried to scare me into leaving before they let the kids in by threatening to call the police.

Tamara: I know that didn't work.

Mama: You know me, don't you? I said, "Call the police Mr. Richardson, call them quick. I'm not breaking any laws and I've worked too long, had too many after-school conversations with you and anybody else who'd listen to turn back now. It's way past time for the name of this school to change and I'm not moving until it does."

Tamara: Oh my God, what happened?

Mumia: From what she told me later that day, Mr. Richardson looked at Granny with that 'I'd kill you now if I could get away with it' look.

Mama: And when he saw that was getting him nowhere, he carefully stepped around me to unlock his office door, walked inside and slammed it.

Mumia: When the first bell rang, letting us kids into school, the first students who saw Granny started passing the message down the long line waiting to pass through the metal detector, until finally it got to me.

Tamara: What did you do, nephew?

Mumia:	At first, I thought somebody was joking with me so I acted like I didn't hear the girl in front of me, but then the principal must have come back out of his office because I heard Granny say loud and clear—
Mama:	I told him he'd better either get back in his office or call the police for real because I was not moving and he'd bet not put his hands on me.
Mumia:	When I heard that, I started asking my friends to help me get to the front so I could go through the metal detector and see for myself what was going on.
Tamara:	How long did it take you?
Mumia:	I have no idea. It was like time stopped and all I could think of was she was in trouble and I needed to get to her as quickly as possible.
Tamara:	Mama, you never told me about any of this. Why?
Mama:	Because I know how you are, that's why. You'd have been ready to get here and get in that principal's behind like he stole something, and what would that have helped?
Tamara:	Are you kidding me? You damn near went Rambo at your grandson's school and you were worried about me cussing out the principal?
Mama:	When you put it like that, I guess I should have let you know. The main thing is, my sit-in took everything to another level fast.
Mumia:	Yep, because once Gran said she wasn't moving and challenged Mr. Richardson to call the police, he started thinking about all the stuff principals think about.
Mama:	Like saving face and making sure the Sun Times didn't find out about this.
Mumia:	He stopped raising his voice to mama, told the security guards to make sure everybody got to homeroom except me.
Tamara:	Why were you allowed to stay?
Mumia:	Because Gran told Mr. Richardson, if he wanted to settle this peacefully, she needed me there as a witness.
Mama:	Once the halls were clear, Mr. Richardson asked me politely if I'd be willing to come into his office to talk about a plan to move forward with changing the name.
Mumia:	After that day, Mr. Richardson acted like a changed man. He went from doing everything he could to resist, to doing all he could to get the entire school community involved.

Mama:	And after another year of meetings, shouting matches, finally getting a majority vote to support the change, we made a comprehensive list of possibilities.
Mumia:	Reduced it down to three: Langston Hughes, Carter G. Woodson, and Ida B. Wells.
Tamara:	Ida B. made it too, good. Mummy, isn't she one of your sheroes?
Mumia:	She is, but to my surprise it was Jake who suggested her.
Tamara:	Okay, then after all of that, what happened to seal the deal?
Mumia:	Mr. Richardson had everyone who was interested in voting come to the school and cast a ballot the old-fashioned way to be sure there was no chance of any foul play.
Tamara:	What do you mean?
Mama:	He means after he had approval from the School Board, Mr. Richardson had the kids make up several large cardboard boxes with slots in the top large enough to put a ballot in, but too small to reach inside. Next, he had his secretary work with them to cut up hundreds of pieces of paper, set up boxes of pencils and from 6:30 a.m. to 6:30 p.m. on November 6th, everybody got a chance to cast their vote. Langston Hughes won hands down and that was it.
Tamara:	I'm impressed.
Mama:	Just goes to show you, when young people decide they want something to change and grown folks join them to help, miracles can happen.
Mumia:	That's what it felt like too, auntie. When the sign people came to replace the name, Mr. Richardson let me and Jake lead the whole school in, "Lift Every Voice and Sing." People started stopping their cars to listen, and some people walked out of their homes across the street and stood on their porches.
Mama:	Good thing is, one man stood on his porch and used his phone to record it.
Mumia:	He sure did. And so far, it's been viewed over a million times. You believe that, auntie?
Tamara:	Sure do, nephew. Will you show me later before I spank that behind on Fortnite?
Mama:	I will never understand what people see in these damn video games. Tee-Tee, you're about as bad as Mummy with this mess.
Tamara:	Mama, how many times—

(*Mumia interrupts.*)

Mumia: I miss mama.

(*They continue talking as if they don't hear him.*)

Tamara: Do I have to tell you…I understand why you don't like video
            games. When you were coming up, you all had cards, chess,
            checkers, and so on. Now we just play different kinds of games,
            and we do it electronically that's all.

Mumia: I remember her smell. Always Chanel No. 5. One time when we
            were working on the number 5 on the way to teaching me to
            count to ten. She sprayed some on the back of her hand and let
            me smell it. I asked her what it was called and she raised her right
            hand, fingers spread apart and said "Five, Mummy, Chanel No. 5.
            It's all I wear."

Mama: (*Beat*) That's nice baby, glad you remember. I believe that's how
            we keep our loved ones alive. We talk about them, say their
            names. Every time we do, they're here with us. I miss her too
            Mummy.

Tamara: Me too, nephew…I bet your dad does too. When's he coming
            home again?

Mumia: I don't know about that, auntie…I guess he does, but he never
            talks about her, and when I bring her up, it seems to piss him off.

Tamara: I think you're wrong about that, nephew. Why would it? He loved
            her almost more than God.

Mumia: I know he did. He's told me that…a lot. But he never tells me
            any stories about her, about their life together before I was born,
            nothing.

Tamara: Maybe it's too hard for him to do that, Mummy…I think it would
            have helped if you'd had a chance to say goodbye to her, but your
            dad doesn't believe in funerals.

Mumia: I don't know if it would have or not, auntie, but thanks for trying
            to convince him. The way I feel, it's like one day I had a mama who
            loved me, sang me to sleep at night, walked me to school, taught
            me to ride a tricycle…then one day I woke up and she had died.

(*Tamara walks over and gives him a hug.*)

Tamara: I understand baby, at least as best I can, I loved her too…Your dad
            will be home soon. I'm praying you'll be able to get him to tell you
            a story or two about your mama this time.

Mumia:	Me too, auntie. All I can do is keep trying.
Mama:	I know you're hurting, grandson, but try to get in tune with your dad's perspective. He's an officer in the Marines, Mummy. He's been away from home more than he's been here for almost 20 years now. There's no telling what's on his mind when you want to talk about your mother…Tee-Tee, he'll be home for Christmas.
Mumia:	I can't wait to see him. We video chat when we can, and he sends me cards and even letters some time, but I still miss him like crazy. Now, he's a worthy adversary for the game. Kicks my butt until he gets tired.
Tamara:	Okay, okay enough signifying about who's worthy, Mummy, it's getting late. Let's go to the guest room and get an hour or two in. Today's Friday, so, no school tomorrow.
Mumia:	Okay, Auntie, I know how bad you want this beat down.

(*Mumia kisses his Grandmother on her forehead.*)

| Mumia: | Night, Gran. |
| Mama: | Night, baby. Exactly two hours, Tamara. I'm setting my alarm to wake me up to check. |

(*Stage fades to black.*)

End of Scene

Act II, Scene II

(*Next Afternoon. It's Saturday and Jeff's in town for the weekend to check on Tamara and her mother. He stops by for a visit. Mama's out grocery shopping and Mumia's at a friend's house. Tamara opens the door.*)

Jeff:	Surprise!
Tamara:	Jeff! What are you doing here?
Jeff:	What do you mean? Are you here?
Tamara:	Yes.
Jeff:	Are you my fiancé?
Tamara:	Yes fool, of course I am.
Jeff:	Then, where else should I be on a Saturday afternoon when you just moved here to help your mama? Come here, Tee.

(They embrace. Tamara's left the door cracked open for some fresh air and Mama walks in and is right up behind them with her arms full of paper grocery bags before they notice her.)

Mama: Boo!

(Jeff and Tamara jump and turn around at the same time.)

Jeff: Ms. Johnson, you scared the shit out of me!

Mama: Good, young man, that's what you get for showing up unannounced on my door step. And Tee-Tee, how many times have I told you 'not' to leave my door open when you're here?

Tamara: Sorry, mama. Did you know the quality of air in most homes is terrible, mainly because people never open their doors or windows to let outside air inside?

(Mama ignores her.)

Mama: Tee-Tee, give me my hug, then ya'll can take these bags to the kitchen for me, while I go upstairs and take my street clothes off.

Tamara: Yes, mama. Come on baby, I'll make us some coffee while you take everything out so I can put it up.

Jeff: Sheez, I've only been here ten minutes and you're already giving me stuff to do.

(Mama responds as she walks upstairs.)

Mama: You may as well get used to it, almost son-in-law, because the time between now and your wedding day is the dress rehearsal for the rest of your life.

Tamara: Come on now, mama, I'm not that bad, am I?

Mama: Who said it was bad?

(Continues up the stairs laughing. Jeff and Tamara enter the kitchen talking.)

Jeff: How are things going, Tee? How's your mother doing?

Tamara: Things are going fine from my end, you know me and Mumia get along fine, and mama was glad to see me.

Jeff: But?

Tamara: Mama's not talking.

Jeff:	Not talking? Since when? Every time I've heard you talking to her by phone, or been around the two of you, you talk to each other so much, it's hard to get a word in, what happened?
Tamara:	Cancer happened again. I think, for all her brave front, she's terrified. And what's so messed up is before I got here, she told me she couldn't wait to talk, but now she wants to talk about everything else. How Mumia's doing, what Ms. So-and-so up the street is planting in her garden, who's messing around with who in church, plus any and everything she can think to ask me about you.
Jeff:	Damn. Surprised and sorry to hear this, Tee. Have you taken your usual direct route and asked her 'why'?
Tamara:	Of course, I have. So many times, I'm trying to think of creative ways to get her to open up.
Jeff:	How does she respond?
Tamara:	That's just it. She doesn't. I'll say something like, 'Good morning mama, can we talk about your surgery?' (*Beat*) Next thing I know, she's stopped what she's doing and left wherever we were in that moment without making a sound. Any other suggestions?
Jeff:	Wish I had some baby, but I don't. You know, I'm lousy at figuring out what will make a woman talk who doesn't want to. Young men, boys, elder brothers, no problem. I mean, look at what happens when for whatever reason you don't want to talk to me about something. Anything I ever tried work?
Tamara:	I see your point. On the other hand, is it possible that because you're so bad at it, you'd be able to get her to open up to you?
Jeff:	Now you're talking crazy. Or as Mumia would say: cra-cra.

(*Mama overhears what Jeff says as she enters the kitchen with her hands in her apron pocket.*)

Mama:	Who's cra-cra?
Tamara:	Nobody you know mama, me and Jeff were talking about one of the young men at Help A Brother Out. Can I pour you a cup of coffee?
Mama:	Yes, Tee-Tee, black please. I'm taking a break from cream and sugar for a while. Trying to lose this extra fifteen pounds before—

(*Mama falls silent, and Jeff and Tamara look at each other briefly as mama starts to prepare lunch for them.*)

Jeff: You don't look like you need to lose weight to me, Ms. Johnson, you look good.

Mama: Thanks, Jeff. That's nice of you.

Tamara: Not nice, mama, true...black it is though. Here...Jeff can I warm yours up?

Jeff: No, I think I'll run a few errands while you and your mother get lunch ready. I'll be back later.

Tamara: Okay, baby. See you in a little while.

Mama: See you later, Jeff. Be careful.

Jeff: I will, Ms. Johnson.

(*Jeff exits. Mama and Tamara, prepare lunch together in silence for a few moments. Tamara's cell phone rings.*)

Tamara: Hello? Jeff, what?!

(*Listens to Jeff.*)

Tamara: You've got to be kidding me.

Mama: What's wrong Tee-Tee?

(*Tamara holds up her hand, a sign for her mother to wait.*)

Tamara: They ran your license plates while you were parked in mama's driveway? Damn, I'm sorry baby.

(*Listens to Jeff.*)

Tamara: I know, it's not the first time...Thank God you learned a long time ago to pick your battles.

(*Listens to Jeff.*)

Tamara: Yep, you're right it could have been worse. See you when you get back. Be careful. Love you more, bye.

Mama: Sorry Tee-Tee. I've lived in this world a lot longer than the two of you, but I'll never get used to the way Black people are treated.

Tamara: I know, mama, but what can we do about it that we're not already doing? At the end of the day, you can't legislate the human heart.

Mama: I know and it is, thanks God, getting better.

Tamara: So true.
Mama: Come on, let's finish getting lunch together so we can eat.
Tamara: Sounds like a plan. I'll play some music while we get it together.

(*After Tamara turns on the radio, Tamara and Mama finish preparing lunch, talking while they work. A song plays that reminds Tamara of her childhood.*)

Tamara: Ooo, that sounds good. Mama, you remember this song?
Mama: Aretha Franklin? Are you kidding? Why do you think you know the song?

(*Tamara does a quick dance step.*)

Tamara: R-E-S-P-E-C-T

(*Mama chimes in.*)

Mama: Take care TCB, sock it to me, sock it to me—

(*Tamara interrupts her by grabbing her quickly to give her a hug.*)

Tamara: Mama, I'm so goddamn worried about you. Please talk to me—I need to talk to you about this, please.

(*Mama disconnects slowly, takes a step back and lifts her blouse, revealing a skin-color-matching tight top that's pressed her breasts flat against her chest.*)

Mama: And what you want me to say Tee-Tee? What? I've been through this mess three times, three...and each time, God's had my back, you've been right here for me, my church family, my friends. I know you're worried, but think about it from my perspective for a minute, know what I mean?

(*Tamara points to her mama's chest.*)

Tamara: What's this? Some kind of preparation for your surgery?
Mama: In a way...a woman in my support group who's already had a double mastectomy recommended I give this a try, so I ordered it online...It's designed to help me get a feel for how my chest is going to look flat as a child's. See it even has suture looking seams where the scars will be.

(Tamara looks closely and notices the seams only slightly darker than the top.)

Tamara: So, what do you think? How does it look?

(She turns her back to Tamara, then speaks as if she's alone, rubbing her hands up and down her chest.)

Mama: It feels like I've never been a mother, never saw my puberty nipples grow and darken, never wore my first beginner bra, felt a lover's caress...then I think about cancer...How it comes into your life like a thief in the dark, makes a home where it's not welcome, grows large enough to be noticed. How it changes you forever cause you never know when it'll come back, stop your life all over again.

(Mama falls silent. Tamara approaches mama from behind and wraps her arms around her chest. Mama begins humming. Tamara starts humming in tune, steps around to her front and gently holds her hands. They continue humming for a few moments.)

Tamara: I'm so sorry, mama. What can I do to help you? Can I fix you something special to eat, will you let me go to the doctor with you this time?

Mama: I know you are, Tee-Tee...I am too. The first time, I spent weeks mad at God, questioning why me, getting mad when I saw other women obviously happy and without breast cancer anywhere near me.

Tamara: I remember, mama...What's different this time?

Mama: I've had it, daughter. That's what's different. I've been down this long road three times before...each time, the doctor's told me I need to stop smoking, you've told me I need to stop, even offered me money to stop one time.

Tamara: What do you mean? Money? I don't remember that.

Mama: You don't remember the bet you kept trying to get me to take? Betting me $100 that I couldn't quit smoking for a week?

Tamara: Oh, that...that wasn't exactly offering you money though was it? I was just trying to get you to stop long enough to have a chance at quitting.

Mama: I know, but like I keep trying to tell you, that kind of stuff would only work if I had any intention of quitting.

Tamara: That's what keeps me up at night. I just don't get why, with all of the scientific evidence that smoking causes cancer, that alone isn't enough to scare you into getting help.

Mama: I'm not sure why, because—

Tamara: Please let me finish. Not to mention all of the people in our family who have died of cancer. Cancer of the lung, throat, pancreas. Big Mama, Grandad, Uncle B, Auntie Julie...not to mention your friends.

Mama: For the last time Tee-Tee. It's real simple. There are two ways to live in this world, you can live each day afraid, not doing the things you enjoy, or you can commit your soul to God and live.

Tamara: What are you talking about, mama?

Mama: I'm saying that I love to smoke, Tee-Tee. It's not something I just do, it's part of my life. I started sneaking Big Mama's cigarettes when I was only 11 years old and from almost the first puff, I loved everything about smoking. The way the cigarette looked hanging from my mouth, the feel of warm smoke in my lungs, blowing through my nostrils...the little boost it gives to my day with a cup of coffee. It helps me cope when I'm stressed out about life's every day stuff—

Tamara: But you know that's not really true, actually cigarettes—

Mama: Girl, will you be quiet and let me finish. I'm not talking about what science says, what doctors say, what you say and think about smoking, you asked me a question, I've answered every way I know how, and the end result is always the same—you claim not to understand where I'm coming from...Some time I get the feeling you want there to be something else behind my desire to smoke, something mysterious, a puzzle you can solve, so I'll stop, but the fact is this—I don't want to. And right about now, the best way you can help your mama is by listening to me and helping me get through what will hopefully be my last visit from cancer in this lifetime...What if someone proved to you that having sex with the person you love would kill you? What would you do?

Tamara: What does that have to do with what we're talking about? Having sex won't kill you unless you have some kind of heart or other health problem.

Mama: Get out of your head for a minute. Would you go your entire life without having sex, so you could live longer?

Tamara: Damn. Never thought about it quite like that.

Mama: Now, see how easy that was? All we had to do was get to the part where everybody deserves to spend their life doing what they love, and if we die because of it, so be it. As my daddy used to say, nobody gets out of here alive, Tee-Tee.

(Tamara pulls out the kitchen chair at the head of the table.)

Tamara: No lie, mama. We're all moving in the same direction...Come and have a seat so I can serve you for a change.

(Mama sits down and Tamara, serves lunch for both of them, then joins her at the table. They hold hands.)

Mama: Lord, bless this food. Amen.
Tamara: That was fast.
Mama: I'm hungry, Tee-Tee, God forgives my brevity. Let's eat.

(Tamara and Mama share food for a few moments.)

Mama: Have you given any more thought to what you want to do about Mummy's questions about his mother?

(Mummy has entered the house quietly, and is about to enter the kitchen from the back when he hears his grandmother's question. He hides behind the wall to listen.)

Tamara: Absolutely not. Mama, we talked about this a long time ago.
Mama: Yes, we did, but that was then and this is now.
Tamara: True, but right off the bat three things make it impossible for either of us to do anything about this.
Mama: Three? I think I got the first one. Not sure about the other two.
Tamara: Okay, what's your reason?
Mama: It's not our story to tell, Tee-Tee. Mummy's father told him what he wanted him to know over 11 years ago. Who are we to correct what he decided to tell his only son?
Tamara: Then why did you ask me the question?
Mama: I don't honestly know, daughter. It's like my lips were moving and words came out that I didn't put there. You ever had that happen to you?

Tamara:	I sure have. Not often, but every now and then. Usually it's because it's something I need to say that hadn't consciously occurred to me yet.
Mama:	Makes sense. Weird thing is, I don't think Mummy should be told the real deal. For what? What will it change?
Tamara:	It will stop him from asking questions we can't answer. And he'll know the truth...Mama?
Mama:	What, baby?
Tamara:	Doesn't it bother you that we're Christians who believe in God's word, yet we're backing up your son and my brother in this lie.
Mama:	Is that better than letting him know that we have no idea where she is? Should we tell him at 15 years old that his mother left, without a note or a word, while his father was overseas? Do you really think he'll be better off?
Tamara:	Who was it that taught me to do the right thing as best you can?
Mama:	I did, but whether or not this is the right thing is complicated.
Tamara:	Since when? Right is right and wrong is wrong. Right?
Mama:	Except when there's more than one way to determine right, like in this case.
Tamara:	This is not a case, mama. Fact is, I don't think I ever got the full story from Johnny. He was so upset and broke up. I'm guessing you did.
Mama:	You're right I did. Regardless of the story, your brother is Mummy's father. He decided when his wife left and he couldn't find her that he'd pretend she died.
Tamara:	Lord have mercy.
Mama:	I hope He will, daughter. At any rate, something else you don't know is that your dad didn't make that decision alone. He came to me crying day after he found out she'd left him and we talked over the best story to tell for Mummy's sake.

(*Mummy can be seen quietly exiting through back door, upset and crying.*)

| Tamara: | Too bad the two of you didn't consider the possibility that at 5 years old, Mummy's memory of his mama would be strong enough to cause him to ask questions to learn more about the life she lived. |
| Mama: | I agree. Right now, we have a young man who's staying out of trouble, doing well in school and has a good relationship with his dad and us. Is the truth more important than letting him |

continue believing she's passed, 'especially' since we have no idea where she is or even if she's alive?

(*As lights fade, Mummy can be heard offstage.*)

Mummy: Hello, Kayla? Can I come over?

End of Scene

Act II, Scene III

(*Mumia knocks on Kayla's side door. He's visibly upset. Her parents aren't home. She opens the door, and he hugs her tight for several moments.*)

Kayla: Mu, what's wrong boo? I've never seen you this upset.

(*Mumia can't speak yet. Shakes his head. Kayla leads him to the couch in the front room. They sit there for a few moments before she turns on her video game, hands him a controller, and they play for a few minutes while she waits for him to start talking. Mumia wins a round.*)

Kayla: Damn, you beat me again, Mu. I hate you.

(*Silence*)

Kayla: Want to play another one?

(*Mumia ignores her and starts talking.*)

Mumia: I feel like my whole life is a lie, Kayla. Everything I thought was true—is bullshit.

Kayla: What you mean baby? How can that be? You got a good dad; your grandmother loves you and isn't your aunt Tee-Tee visiting right now? What's wrong? You know you can tell me anything.

Mumia: I know I can. It's not you it's me. I don't even know where to start. Dad raised me to keep stuff that happens at the house, in the house. Not to air our dirty clothes out in the world.

Kayla: Yeah, I was raised that way too, but this is just me and you, so what's going on?

Mumia:	I got home a little early from school today and since I forgot my key in my other pants, I went to the back door and got the key my grandmother keeps hidden in case we need it...I heard auntie and granny talking in the kitchen. Granny asked auntie 'when' she was going to talk to me about what really happened to mama.
Kayla:	What?
Mumia:	Yep. I stopped and hid behind the wall beside the doorway to listen. K, everything my dad told me, everything my grandmother and auntie had told me over the years is a lie.
Kayla:	You mean your mother didn't die suddenly while she was away on a cyber security consulting gig in Paris?
Mumia:	No.

(*He puts his head in his hands. Kayla comforts him.*)

Kayla:	I'm so sorry, Mu. What else did they say?
Mumia:	They said mama disappeared. Left on one of her regular trips to develop cyber security for clients and just never came back. No letter, no phone call, no email...nothing.
Kayla:	I'm confused.
Mumia:	All these years. I've been asking God to give her a hug at night, talking to her, telling her I'll see her soon.
Kayla:	Soon? You planning something you want to tell me about? We're only 15, Mu.
Mumia:	No, K. I didn't mean it like that. I can't imagine anything that would make me take my life. I think about time as being on an endless continuum. It's not like a straight line that begins and ends, it's more like one continuous circle, some of us are born, others join our ancestors.
Kayla:	I don't know what the hell you're talking about, but I'm trying.
Mumia:	The short of it is, people made up how time works, and to me, even if I live 100 years, that's only a moment in the afterlife where spirits have shed the body like old clothes and exist in eternity.
Kayla:	Where did they say she is?
Mumia:	While I was standing there biting my tongue, I heard my grandmother tell auntie they still don't know.
Kayla:	Really?
Mumia:	Yep...according to granny, dad and she discussed what to do and decided that since they had no idea where she was, it would be

better to pretend she had died overseas on a business trip. A couple weeks later he left me with my grandmother, shipped back out and that was it.

Kayla: Lord help us please...that sounds like some mess you'd see in a movie, Mu.

Mumia: No lie, Kayla.

Kayla: I'm so sorry this happened...I wish I could say something that would help, but I'm damn near speechless.

Mumia: I know you feel me...Thanks K.

Kayla: What are you going to do now?

Mumia: No idea. I'm hoping you can hide me here for a few days, so I can have some time to think.

Kayla: Wish I could, but mama and daddy are way too nosy for me to try that. I can't even have my computer or phone in my room at night, and mama sticks her head in my door at least a couple of times to check on me. According to her, she's been doing that since I was a baby. Sorry, Mu.

Mumia: (*Beat*) All my life my dad, granny, auntie, everybody has always stressed the importance of family...that without family we're nothing. Dad has beat me over the head with being honest, keeping it real between us...Now, that's not to say I don't occasionally tell a lie. For example, I don't have a girlfriend since I'm not allowed to, so they don't know about me and you, but I do my best to tell them what's up...always.

Kayla: I feel that too, Mu...you haven't been around them, but I've told you about how close my family is...we have people all over the country, and haven't missed having a family reunion in 85 years. I can't even imagine how you feel.

Mumia: I know Kayla, thanks. At least I have one person I can talk to...I almost wish.

(*He falls silent.*)

Kayla: Wish what?

Mumia: You know your uncle and his crew have been trying to recruit me into the D-Dogs since I turned 12, right?

Kayla: I do. And I know you always told B-Roll you didn't need another family.

Mumia: That's right. What I didn't tell him was, my dad would kill me if I even dreamed about joining a gang, all the work he's put into helping me get the best start in life he can provide. Catholic

	school, art lessons, baseball...he even made me join the summer reading club at the library for the first two years, and I've been signing up on my own ever since.
Kayla:	How many times have you not been number one?
Mumia:	Never so far. Always makes my dad and grandmother happy. Plus, dad puts $100 into my college fund each summer I win as encouragement to keep it up.
Kayla:	Mu, I hate to cut our time short, but you need to think about what you're going to do now cause my parents will be home soon and you can't be here.
Mumia:	What do you think about the D-Dogs?
Kayla:	What I think isn't important. I'm not a young man, have never been recruited by a girl gang. Mainly because I already whooped everybody in the G-Girls back in elementary school, so they don't even think about messing with me...On the other hand, I love my uncle B-Roll and to him the D-Dogs are like a fraternity, except fraternities are legal. When he lost his dad in Iraq, his mother had a nervous breakdown and he came to stay with us till he got grown. My uncle is not only the leader, he wouldn't hesitate to go down for any one of them. Plus, they're not into violence.
Mumia:	Unless another gang tries to come through our neighborhood wearing another gang's colors.
Kayla:	Which hasn't happened much since I was a little girl. For the most part, they hang out, and travel out of town together.
Mumia:	And they have each other's backs like family always should, right?
Kayla:	Definitely.
Mumia:	I could use a family right about now...can you call your uncle and ask him to come and get me? I need to talk.
Kayla:	What? Hell naw. Are you kidding me, Mu? Or are you so hurt and stressed out that you've lost what's left of your mind?
Mumia:	No, I'm not kidding...My mind might be thinking clearer right now than it ever has.
Kayla:	Now, I know you've lost it.
Mumia:	What's the problem? You were just telling me how much you love your uncle; about how much good the D-Dogs do in the neighborhood.
Kayla:	Yeah, I do love him and you already knew about the good they do around here, but that never made you want to join before. You mean to tell me you're willing to make a change that could affect your whole life, right now, without taking some time to think?
Mumia:	I've been thinking on the way over here.

Kayla: I don't mean for a few hours when you've just had your whole world turned upside down. I mean at least a few days, a week, maybe more.

Mumia: Why should I? My family's betrayed me. Had me thinking mama's dead and she's not.

Kayla: You're right and I feel you on that, but don't you think they at least deserve the opportunity to explain beyond what you overheard. Don't you think you should have a chance to talk to your dad, get his side of the story, before you do something you might regret for the rest of your life? You're not a follower, Mummy, you're a thinker, a dreamer, somebody I think is destined to make a difference in this world...Please, Mu.

(*Mummy sits silently for a few moments with his head in his hands.*)

Mumia: My dad always tells me that.

Kayla: What?

Mumia: That I'm destined for greatness...Been telling me that since I was a little boy, when I had no idea what he was even talking about, but it felt good. He's always been so proud of me.

Kayla: See, I'm not the only one. You've never told me much about what you and your dad talk about, but you've always shared how much you admire and love him...that the last thing the two of you say to each other is, "I love you." So, bottom line, you might leave here deciding to find B-Roll on your own, but that's the only way cause I'm not ever going to call him for you. If you want to know what I think you should do—

Mumia: Did you hear me ask you?

Kayla: No, and I don't care. I care about you, so I'm telling you anyway.

Mumia: Okay, what?

Kayla: I think you should see how fast you can get to the rapid station and take your behind home. Apologize for being so late, take the consequences for not getting home on time, then when you're ready, talk to your dad first to get his side of the story, find a way to tell him how you feel, forgive him and your family and keep moving forward with your life...My two cents.

(*Mummy looks deep into her eyes for a few moments, and reaches over to give her a hug. Kayla breaks away.*)

Kayla:	Mu, I have something to tell you.
Mumia:	Okay, tell me what? Come one now, I got enough on my head. Whatever it is, spit it.
Kayla:	Mu, I have 'nothing' to back this up, but I've always had a feeling my uncle hasn't ben completely honest about what the D-Dogs are about.
Mumia:	What? You just told me what you know. What else could there be?
Kayla:	No idea. I'm just telling what my gut has said at times when I've been around him. Look, I care about you a lot Mu, and I just don't want you to get all tied up in something you weren't thinking about messing with as recently as yesterday...Would you please just go home and at least see how you feel in the morning and call me?
Mumia:	Okay, okay, K...I will. You're right I'm blessed to have my dad and granny and auntie in my life. You've given me a lot to think about...I'm glad I called you.

(Kayla stands up, reaches out her arms, and when Mummy stands, neither of them notices Mummy's cell phone slip out of his pocket onto the couch, as Kayla gives him a hug and a deep kiss.)

Kayla:	I'm glad you called me too. Now, please go. It's time for my parents to pull up in the driveway.
Mumia:	I understand. Alright I'm on my way straight to the rapid. Glad it's not too far from here.
Kayla:	Night, Mu.
Mumia:	Night, K. Talk to you tomorrow.

End of Scene

Act II, Scene IV

(Same night. Mummy's lost in thought. It's after 10 o'clock and the streets are fairly quiet. Very few cars pass him, and as he gets closer to the rapid, some streetlights are out and he's in the dark as he sees the lights of the station up ahead. Suddenly, he's approached from behind and cracked upside the head. Two Black men grab him and rush him into the back of a black van waiting on the street. B-Roll is driving.)

B-Roll: Duct tape his mouth and make sure you zip-tie his hands and feet. He can fight and I don't want him waking up and making noise before we get to the spot.

(*The two men do what they're told without a sound, and the van disappears into the night.*)

(*Early next morning. Mummy wakes up in a brightly lit basement. He's disoriented, stripped down to his underwear and alone. He sees a large screen on the back wall filled with Zoom screen images of older men looking him over carefully. He sees a laptop on the right wall lying on a table that holds a steaming hot cup of coffee and a bottle of water.*)

Mumia: Help! Help! Please somebody help me!

(*B-Roll enters from the back door behind Mumia's head and smacks him across the mouth so hard that Mumia's head turns and blood spurts out.*)

B-Roll: Shut up, mothafucka! Can't nobody hear you. I got you.

(*Mumia shuts his mouth and looks B-Roll straight in the eye. He's scared but knows not to show it.*)

Mumia: B-Roll, what are you doing? I told you before, I'm not joining the D-Dogs.
B-Roll: And I heard you loud and clear. This ain't about joining, it's about business.
Mumia: Business? What are you talking about? Who are all these old men?
B-Roll: I'm about to show you.

(*He takes a piece of duct tape and puts it across Mumia's mouth, then walks over to the computer screen and addresses the men waiting on the large screen.*)

B-Roll: Sorry about the delay, guys. I got back as quick as I could.

(*The men acknowledge him without speaking, watching Mumia intently. When B-Roll gets to the table with the computer, he remains standing to address the men.*)

B-Roll: Now, let's get down to business. I told you this one would be special. Notice his smooth skin, handsome face. Look at his body.
You can tell he works out. Plus, he's smart and talented too. Excel-
lent student, video gamer, respectful. Once he realizes he has no
choice, he should give your group months of pleasure.

(*Mumia begins struggling in his seat. Terrified, he stops as the men begin to bid.
B-Roll takes a seat behind the computer.*)

B-Roll: Okay, each of you has shopped with me before. This is a silent
auction. Bidding starts at one thousand dollars.

(*The sounds of bids reaching B-Roll's computer are heard for a couple of
minutes.*)

B-Roll: Bidding's at $3,000. Anybody else? Going once, going twice, last
call? Okay, sold! #369, Cash App me and I'll have your purchase
on its way no later than midnight today. Thanks everybody. Will
be in touch in a couple of months. Till then, enjoy.

(*B-Roll ends the Zoom Meeting. Speaks to Mummy who's so terrified he's crying
and trembling*)

B-Roll: Ain't no use in crying now, Mummy. This shit is a wrap. I'll be
back.

(*B-Roll exits the room and turns out the overhead lights, leaving only a single
lamp on.*)

End of Scene

Act II, Scene V

(*It's after dinner time the same day. As far as Mumia's aunt and grandmother are
concerned, he hasn't been home, and they sit at the dining room table talking and
calling folks to see if he's there.*)

Mama: Hello? Hello? Oh, hi, yes, Ms. Robinson, this is Mumia's grandmother, is he there?

(*Listening*)

Mama: No? Well, have you seen him at all today?

(*Listening*)

Mama: What?! Sorry, sorry to scream in your ear. It's just that Mumia
           is rarely late and he usually lets me know if he's going to be,
           because he knows I worry, and if he left there at around 5 o'clock,
           it's almost 9 o'clock now and I'm scared.

(*Listening, as Tamara hangs up her cell phone and looks shocked.*)

Mama: Yes, I know Ms. Robinson, our kids can be thoughtless some
           time. Yes, I know you're closing. Please add my grandson to your
           prayers tonight.

(*Listening*)

Mama: Okay, thanks, Ms. Robinson. Goodnight.

(*Tamara quickly walks over to her and reaches for her hand. They sit together
praying silently with their eyes closed for a few moments.*)

Tamara: Mama, I just gave it to God. I can't let myself think anything's
           happened to Mummy.
Mama: Me either, and I gave it to God too, but I think we need to give God
           a hand. Call Jeff and tell him what's going on, Tee-Tee. Have him
           meet us here so we can figure out the best way to find Mummy.

(*Tamara dials Jeff's number on her cell phone.*)

Tamara: Jeff? Baby, I need you. Mummy's missing and he's never not been
           in this house by curfew.

(*Listening*)

Tamara: We've already called everybody we could think of, his friends, Ms.
           Robinson, the desk clerk at the library he's always talking to, Mr.
           Wilson at the Community Center.

(*Listening*)

Tamara: We've run out of people to call, Jeff. We need to start looking.

(*Listening*)

Tamara: Okay, we'll be here waiting. Please hurry.
Mama: Let's go upstairs and look in his room while we wait, maybe we'll
             find something to help us figure this out.

(*A few moments later in Mumia's room, they both move to different parts, looking
under his bed, at some of the books in the overloaded book case against the wall,
etc.*)

Tamara: Have you ever seen a boy's room look this neat in your life?
Mama: This must be your first time in Mummy's room.
Tamara: It is. What would I be in his room for? Like most teenaged boys
             I've ever known including my brother, his daddy, they never want
             us in their rooms.
Mama: So true, Tee-Tee. A lot of grown men feel that way too.
Tamara: Including Jeff, but—

(*They say it together.*)

Mama&Tam: But they don't have any choice because nobody's man cave is safe.

(*They take a moment to give each other high fives.*)

Tamara: Anyway, a room this neat is both good and bad news.
Mama: What do you mean?
Tamara: Good news, because I'm glad Mummy's developed good house-
             keeping habits, and bad news because there's no junk or mess to
             look under.
Mama: What about all of these books? What's he been reading?
Tamara: According to his bookcase, he's been reading almost nothing but
             books on how to get better at his two favorite online games Fort-
             nite and Chess.
Mama: Really? That's it?
Tamara: Yep, along with a few classics of course. The Autobiography of
             Malcolm X, The Mis-Education of the Negro and The Bluest Eye.

Mama: Funny how your eyes zeroed in on the three books you gave him
             for his birthday, which also happen to be three of your all-time
             favorites.
Tamara: Exactly. Nice to see he still has them. I'm impressed.
Mama: Bottom line, I don't see anything in here to worry me in the least.
             Let's go back downstairs and wait for Jeff.
Tamara: Okay, maybe somebody will call us back while we're waiting.

*(They start walking down the steps and the doorbell rings. Tamara answers the
door as Mama stands waiting)*

Tamara: Jeff, damn, you got here fast. Thanks, baby.

(Jeff talking fast.)

Jeff: What's going on? Where's Mummy? Has anyone heard from him
             yet? Have you called the police? Have you been out looking?
Tamara: Jeff, Jeff. Calm down baby. Take a breath. Come on, let me get you
             a drink.

(Jeff, grabs her hand gently and pulls her to him)

Jeff: The last thing I want right now is a drink. Tell me what happened
             so we can find your nephew.
Mama: And my grandson. I'm so glad you're here. Now, hurry up and tell
             him what we know, Tee-Tee, time is wasting.
Tamara: Jeff's, there's not much to tell. Mummy didn't come home from
             school. Mama called the library just before closing time and
             spoke to Ms. Robinson, who said she'd seen him when he left the
             library at around 5 o'clock.
Jeff: Did he say anything to her?
Mama: No. At least if he did, she didn't mention it.
Tamara: Good question, Jeff, but if he had I'd be surprised. Ms. Robinson's
             nice, and I know she's crazy about Mummy, but she's also nosy as
             hell and he'd never tell her where he was going.
Jeff: Did you check his room, to see if anything's there that would
             give us a clue to something he might be doing that you two don't
             know?
Mama: We sure did. We just came back downstairs, right before you rang
             the doorbell.
Jeff: You find anything?

Tamara:	Nope, his room's neat as a straight pin. All we found were some interesting books on mastering Fortnite and on-line Chess.
Jeff:	You mind if I go up and take a second look?
Mama:	Not at all. Take your time.

(*Jeff, heads upstairs to look as Mama goes to the bar, pours two stiff drinks and hands one to Tamara.*)

Mama:	You think he'll find anything?
Tamara:	No idea, but it's worth a shot because right now, we don't have a clue.
Mama:	And no idea who else to call to try to get one, either.

(*They sit for a few seconds sipping their drinks, lost in thought. Jeff heads back down the steps with a tin box.*)

Tamara:	Hey, what's that?
Mama:	And where'd you find it?
Jeff:	Wait a minute, ladies. Give me a chance to sit down and I'll show you.

(*He takes a seat between them on the couch and opens the box. He removes a framed picture of Mumia's mother and sets it facing the audience on the coffee table. Mama picks it up while he removes a Black, male GI Joe figure and a stuffed toy lion—the last thing his mother gave him. Tamara quietly picks up the GI Joe.*)

Mama:	I've been wondering what happened to this picture of my sweetie-pie...Used to sit on the nightstand beside my bed.
Tamara:	It sure did, I remember, mama. In fact, you have several copies of this same picture of auntie, don't you?
Mama:	Yes, I do, Tee-Tee...It's her graduation picture from college. That was an amazing day. She was so happy...she smiled for so long, I was afraid her face would freeze like that.
Jeff:	Mummy must have loved it too, if he took the risk of stealing it from you.
Mama:	Wonder why he didn't just ask me for it? I'd have had one made up for him.
Jeff:	Who can say why kids do what they do? He may not have thought past he wanted it to remember his mama by, and grabbed it. No harm, no foul right?
Tamara:	What do you mean?

Mama:	I think he means, regardless of how he got it, we're not supposed to know he has it, so I can't say anything, right?
Jeff:	Exactly.
Mama:	Okay, I promise, I won't.
Tamara:	Me too.
Jeff:	Why are you holding his GI Joe, Tee?
Tamara:	Because this was Mummy's favorite toy...His dad gave it to him for his fourth Christmas.
Jeff:	Fourth? How do you remember how old he was after all these years?

(*Tamara stands GI Joe up on the coffee table.*)

| Tamara: | Jack hated to do shopping of any kind...When it came to Mummy and his wife, I was his secret shopper. He'd wire me the money when he was away on duty and when he was at home, he'd give me cash...On each occasion I'd waste time asking him if he had any ideas, and by the time he said 'no' I was already making a list of possibilities in my head, looking for a paper and pen to write them down. |
| Mama: | Just goes to show, you can always learn something new about your own family. Tee-Tee, how come you never told me this? |

(*Tamara gives her a look that says 'you know why' and continues.*)

Tamara:	Jack wasn't able to come home for Mummy's fourth Christmas, it was the one time of year he did his best to make it home, but a new series of attacks in Afghanistan made that impossible... plus, communication was messed up, so I didn't hear from him until early Christmas Eve morning...Me and mama, and Mummy's mother had already bought our gifts and hid them, but the one thing I hadn't been able to find was a GI Joe. At the time, it had regained popularity and not a single store had one.
Jeff:	Then how did you find one at the last minute?
Mama:	I bet she called my ex.

(*Tamara's surprised.*)

| Tamara: | You're right, I did. How did you know? |
| Mama: | I didn't, but I'm guessing he's still a hoarder and if *I* was looking for something nobody else had, he's the first person I'd call. |

Tamara: Well, you hit that nail, mama. Not only did Henry have 'one' GI Joe, he had nine of them.

Mama: Not surprised...he always did hoard stuff other people would want to buy, even though I've never known him to sell anything.

Tamara: And of course, he didn't sell me this either...He was happy to see me. Gave it to me on my promise that I'd come to see him more often, with one of your egg custard pies.

Mama: What...So that's why you all of a sudden developed a taste for my egg custard any time you came to see me. I just figured you wanted something different for a change.

Tamara: Now, you know mama. I was keeping my word to my stepdad... remember the look on Mummy's face when he opened the box?

Mama: Not exactly, but I do remember he used to sleep with it every night...until...

Tamara: His dad came into his room one night and took it from him, telling him he was too old to sleep with dolls.

Mama: Now, I *do* remember that. Your father left the next day and wasn't there to hear Mummy cry himself to sleep every night for weeks without his toy...I couldn't go against my son's word, but it hurt to hear him suffer, especially so young.

(*Jeff picks up the lion.*)

Jeff: Looks like it's still important to him, because other than his journal, this worn out lion was the only other thing in the box

(*Tamara reaches for the lion.*)

Tamara: Mummy's mama bought this for him when he was a baby. Used to break the rules about limiting the possibility of SIDS by keeping him on his back, in an empty crib every night, because she didn't want him to sleep alone.

Mama: That lion was like that Charlie Brown character's blanket...what was his name?

Jeff: Linus?

Mama: Yep. He took it everywhere. Loved that thing. Finally stopped on his own when he was about ten. Didn't know he still had it.

Tamara: What's he been writing about? And where did you find the box?

Jeff: Where is a secret I'll take to my grave. It's a male thing, baby. When he comes home, I'm sure he'll keep it in the same place and if I told you, you'd be able to find it. As for his writing, looks

like he's been keeping a journal since he was about nine years old
if the numbers and dates at the top of each page mean anything.

Mama: What do you mean?

Jeff: This is journal number 18, so I'm guessing he's been doing this for
a while.

Tamara: Okay, but again, 'what's' he been writing about baby?

Jeff: I've only skimmed through it and read a few entries, but it boils
down to three things: His mother, his relationship with his dad,
and...his girlfriend.

(*Mama and Tamara together.*)

M&T: His what?

Jeff: You heard me. His girlfriend...Come on now, ladies think back to
when the two of you were 15. Did either of you have a boyfriend?

(*Tamara looks at her mother.*)

Tamara: I plead the fifth.

Mama: And I'll plead to acting like I didn't hear that question, but I get
your point. Neither of my kids were allowed to have them until
they turned sixteen and I wasn't either. So, I guess I can understand why Mummy didn't tell me or his dad, but what am I supposed to do, now that I know?

Jeff: Nothing, because you don't.

Mama: What do you mean?

Jeff: I mean I've just helped the two of you dig deep into Mummy's
business. This box is like opening parts of his life he's been keeping to himself...He can't know anything about this.

Tamara: I agree, Jeff...Besides mama, you know if you and Jack forbid him
from seeing whoever this is, it will just make him want to get
closer to her.

Mama: Okay, okay, I agree...Can you at least read something he wrote
about her.

(*Jeff, opens the journal, selects a page and reads briefly.*)

Jeff: 'Yesterday, I watched K walk away from me at the end of her
street. She can't have a boyfriend either so I have to stop at the

corner. I always wait till she gets in the house safe, but for some reason today, she got halfway down the block and turned around to run back to me. She dropped her book bag and wrapped her arms around me so tight, kissed me so deep I felt like I was losing it. I put one foot between her legs, picked her up and before I knew it, I'd said "I love you, K, will you marry me?"'

Tamara: Awwww...

Mama: Aw what? Did you hear what that boy wrote?

Jeff: Come on now, try not to get too upset. Don't you remember puppy love?

Mama: Puppy love, my dead auntie's behind. She used to say, 'Niece, puppy love is for dogs, when boys say "I love you" at that age it has nothing to do with pets.'

Tamara: Mama, you're right it doesn't, but we all know Mummy's not seriously thinking about getting married, even if he could and he can't.

Jeff: Right, he's just being a boy who's discovering physical things about himself for the first time and doesn't know how to deal with it...If I were you, I wouldn't give this a second thought.

Tamara: Especially since there's absolutely nothing you can do about it, mama. You can't tell his dad and you can't let Mummy know you know. Can we try to forget about it for now, and concentrate on getting him back home?

Mama: You're right, daughter. Jeff, any ideas?

Jeff: I do, but first I want to point out what I didn't find in that box.

Tamara: Which was?

Jeff: No cigarettes, joints, pills, porn...

Mama: Alright, almost-son-in-law, that's enough, we get it.

Tamara: Yes, we do and in this age of social media exposure, that's saying a lot.

Mama: Still a good young man. Thanks God.

Jeff: Ditto that. Now if we can just find him...I know somebody local who I'm certain can help us, but I have to go to him, can't talk about this on the phone.

(He begins placing everything back in the box, gets up to return it to its hiding place.)

Tamara: Alright, baby. Come right back as soon as you can. You know we'll be here worrying.

Mama:	In the meantime, let's go in the kitchen. I'll make a fresh pot of coffee and you can heat up some of the apple cobbler I have in the freezer.
Tamara:	I don't feel hungry, mama.
Mama:	I know, I know. Let's see how you feel when you smell it nice and hot.

(They exit to the kitchen as Jeff rushes down the steps, grabs his coat, pauses to send a quick text and exits.)

End of Scene

Act II, Scene VI

(Jeff is sitting at his desk in the headquarters of HABO, located in the neighborhood where he first met Brother, the man who inspired his non-profit. He's sitting there drinking a cup of hot tea to help steady his nerves. Someone knocks quietly on the door. He gets up to answer.)

| Jeff: | Who is it? |
| Brother: | It's Don't-wait-for-Superman, mofo. Open the door. |

(Jeff opens the door and they embrace.)

Jeff:	Brother, damn, you got here fast...thanks, man.
Brother:	Course, you know how we do. I know this will sound weird, but I could pick up the vibe in your text.
Jeff:	Right about now, nothing sounds crazy. We can't find Mummy.

(Brother immediately stands up as if on high alert.)

Brother:	What? Since when? And before you start, be brief Jeff. Give me the short version.
Jeff:	He didn't come home from school. Tee and her mama called everybody they could think of to try and locate him, but the last person to see him was that library lady, just before closing time. Since then, crickets.
Brother:	Lord have mercy. Not like him. What else?
Jeff:	He has a girlfriend.

Brother:	And?
Jeff:	His mama and aunt just found out today, when I found his secret box in his room, and read part of his journal.
Brother:	Understood, but what's that got to do with where he is?
Jeff:	Don't know, but my experience has been, if a child's keeping something from you, that's a good place to start when there's trouble.
Brother:	True that, Jeff.

(*Silence*)

Jeff:	Mummy's life for your thoughts. Why are you quiet?
Brother:	Bottom line. Only three possibilities I can think of, if what you've shared with me about your girl's nephew is true. Either he ran away for some reason, somebody snatched him for trafficking, or...we won't talk about the third option yet.
Jeff:	You don't have to say it...It's the only option that's been on my mind, since I heard he was missing.
Brother:	Let's start with the most likely, when you talking about a 15-year-old dude. What did you say his girlfriend's name is?
Jeff:	Not sure. He calls her the letter 'K' in his journal, but that could mean a lot of names.
Brother:	It could also be short for "Kay" or something like that. Jeff?
Jeff:	What? What's up.
Brother:	We don't talk about my past much, but I think you know even though you helped me get my shit together a while back, I still know everybody who's doing damn near anything around here.
Jeff:	What are you thinking?
Brother:	I'm thinking D-Dogs. B-Roll their leader to be exact. If I remember correctly, he has a niece named Kayla. Calls her Kay-Kay.
Jeff:	How old is she?
Brother:	Fifteen. (*Beat*) Let me get with B-Roll and one other dude I know from the neighborhood.
Jeff:	Who is that?
Brother:	Police detective friend, who doesn't want folks to know he still knows me. What's important is we're close as blood, and from-time-to-time, we help each other. Nowadays it's rare, but he never lets me down and I'm tellin' you whatever it is, he will help get your nephew back.

Jeff: I appreciate you Brother, but before you leave can you tell me anything about B-Roll?

(*Brother sits back down, leans in and lowers his voice.*)

Brother: Yep. I can tell you he's not somebody you want to fuck with. Most people in the neighborhood would say I'm crazy if they heard me say that, but bottom line is...I don't care what they say...he's dangerous.

Jeff: How do you know?

Brother: The only difference between him and any other gangsta I know is, he don't shit where he lives.

Jeff: Meaning, he does his dirt away from home.

Brother: Far away from home and I'm not even sure of details because, keeping it real, I don't want to know. Tell you what though...I've never known B-Roll to work a legitimate job, him and his Dogs hang out in various parts of the neighborhood all day everyday for weeks at a time, helping elders with their groceries, cutting grass, cleaning up empty lots, maybe a brief ass-kicking or two on occasion, to keep their rep straight, then they disappear for a month or so at a time.

Jeff: Okay, but so far you haven't told me anything that explains why you think he's dangerous.

Brother: One time when we was about 16, 17, and he'd just started the D-Dogs, his mama called him while we were hanging out together at the Q Community Center. It was a short conversation, but I'd never seen that look on B-Roll's face before. He went from looking like a teenaged kid just beginning to smell himself, to a grown man with kill in his eyes...When I asked him what was wrong, he just turned as if his head didn't have a neck, mumbled something about having something to take care of, and he was gone...I didn't see him for about two weeks and by then I'd heard the story, but me and him never talked about it.

Jeff: What story? What happened, Bro?

Brother: Short of it is this: His mama told him her boyfriend had pushed her down in the driveway when they were arguing...Next thing anybody know, the man disappeared and nobody's heard from him since.

Jeff: Damn...And you think B-Roll had something to do with that?

Brother:	Don't think—know. Sure as I know my name and who my daddy is—he made it happen. After that, his mama stayed single till she died late last year.
Jeff:	Damn...sorry to hear that, but the only thing I can think of right now is please find Mumia, for me Brother. I'd call the police...
Brother:	No police, come on now.
Jeff:	Will you let me finish. Plus, didn't you just tell me you have a friend who's a police detective?
Brother:	Yes, I did, but there's a big difference between the po-lice you know and the ones you don't know.
Jeff:	I understand, Brother. Just please tell me what I can do to help you find him as soon as possible.
Brother:	You can hang out here or go back to your girl's mama's house and wait till you hear from me. That's it...Know that as far as I'm concerned, it's like whoever it is took my son, if I had one. I'm on it, and it shouldn't take long, okay?
Jeff:	I know you got my back. Please hurry.

(*They embrace and Brother exits.*)

End of Scene

Act II, Scene VII

(*Local bar. B-Roll is seated at the bar drinking a beer when Brother enters.*)

B-Roll: Well, I'll be damned, long time no see B, how you doin?

(*Brother approaches and they give each other neighborhood dap.*)

Brother:	I'm doing okay. Keeping out the way, doing my best to mind my own business, you know what's up.
B-Roll:	I do. Miss seeing you around at night, but I know you stay close to the HABO center as much as possible. I don't know him, but I hear that dude Jeff is getting the paper from white folks to do some good work over there.
Brother:	He is and not just from white folks into philanthropy and non-profits either. Black people and others with money donate too.
B-Roll:	That's good...What brings you this way tonight. What's going on?

Brother: Glad you asked...Don't want to seem like I only come around when something's wrong, but there is. I need your help.

B-Roll: If you need my help, it's serious. Whatever it is, spit it.

Brother: Jeff's fiancé's nephew Mumia is missing since early evening and he's never late. I know you know everything that goes down around here. Have you seen him?

B-Roll: Nope, I haven't...I know him, have seen him around the neighborhood, believe I may have tried to recruit him a couple of times, but he wasn't having none of it, so that was it.

(Brother looks B-Roll in the eye for several seconds.)

Brother: Okay, something don't feel right, but I have to trust you're telling me the truth. Been down too many roads with you, back in the day B.

B-Roll: I feel the same. The reason you probably don't feel right is you know your woman's nephew is missing and thought I'd know where he was if anybody did. Now, you're back to square one...let me put some feelers out. See if something slipped by me. If I hear anything, I'll holla immediately.

Brother: Appreciate that, B...Let me keep it moving. I need to give Jeff and Tee an update. Praying whoever his girlfriend is, that's where he's at.

(They give each other neighborhood dap. Brother leaves and stops not far from the bar to call his childhood police detective friend.)

(Listening)

Brother: Hi you doin' Ronnie?

(Listening)

Brother: Who is this? Oh, okay, you joking.

(Listening)

Brother: No lie, it has been a minute. We can catch up later. Right now, I have an emergency and need to get with you asap...Remember me telling you about Jeff's fiancé?

(*Listening*)

Brother: She has a nephew and I think B-Roll has him.

(*Listening*)

Brother: 'Cause I just left him. Asked him if he'd seen Mummy and even though he told me 'No,' I've been playing poker with that negro too long not to know when he's lying. If he don't have him, he knows who does.

(*Listens*)

Brother: Nope, I just need you to find out where. I'll take it from there.

(*Listens*)

Brother: Yep, the usual place. See you in 20 minutes.

Act II, Scene VIII

(*Low light. B-Roll approaches in shadow, pushing Mumia in front of him, holding the rope around his waist tight. Mumia's mouth is duct taped and his hands are duct taped in front of him. Brother approaches quickly from behind and puts a gun to B-Rolls head*)

Brother: Don't say shit. Just let him go right the fuck now or I'm gon' end you.

(*B-Roll quickly lets go of the rope, Brother snatches Mumia off to the side, takes B-Rolls gun from the back of his waist.*)

Brother: Lay on the ground face down and count to 100 before you move and don't ever fuck with Jeff or any of his people again. You feel me?

(*B-Roll nods his head and Brother and Mumia exit quickly.*)

End of Act II

Act III, Scene I

(Brother takes Mummy to Tamara's mama's house and rings the doorbell. Jeff answers with Tamara and her mother right behind. Mummy rushes forward and is surrounded by their hugs as Brother and Jeff have a moment.)

Brother: Told you I'd bring him home safe.

Jeff: Thank you, man. I can't even begin to tell you what this means to me.

Brother: You don't have to tell me nothing. I'm just glad I was able to keep my word. We'll talk tomorrow at the house.

(They embrace.)

Jeff: See you then, Brother.

(Brother exits and Jeff turns to join the others, who are hugged up and seated so close together on the couch he has to make space to squeeze in beside Tamara.)

Jeff: Sounds a lot better in here now than it did a few minutes ago.

Mama: I'd tell you to be quiet, except I'm so happy to have this boy back, I can't do anything but smile, and thank God.

Tamara: Say that again, for me.

(They hug Mumia from both sides again.)

Tamara: Mummy, you've hardly said a word since you got back. How are you feeling?

Mummy: I don't have words for it Auntie...I'm just glad. Glad to be alive, and back home.

Tamara: Alive? What? What happened?

Mama: Wait a minute, now. Mummy, before you start talking, let's go to the kitchen. I know everybody's hungry, let me fix something to eat.

(They exit to the kitchen hugged up, happy Mummy's okay.)

End of Scene

Act III, Scene II

(Early morning. Mama enters wearing her hat and coat. Tamara's with her, carrying a large suitcase.)

Tamara:	Mama, this thing is heavy. What do you have in here?
Mama:	None of your business, Tee-Tee. I have what I need for the next two days.
Tamara:	You mean for the next few days, mama. The doctor told you that a double mastectomy requires more time in the hospital. They want to make sure you're okay before they send you home.
Mama:	I know, I heard what he said. I'm saying, I'm coming home the morning of the third day. Can you please humor me just this once?
Tamara:	Yes, mama. Sorry, didn't mean to upset you. I know you have enough on your mind. Are you ready?
Mama:	No, but let's go.
Tamara:	Can we pray first?
Mama:	I appreciate the offer, but me and God had a long conversation this morning, before I woke you up. I'm fine. Let's get out of here before I change my mind.

(They exit the front door and head to the hospital.)

(Later that evening. Tamara and Mummy are sitting on the couch playing video games on their phones. Doorbell rings and it's Jeff. Tamara gives Mummy the eye letting him know to disappear. He puts his phone in his pocket and exits the house from the back door, as Tamara answers to let Jeff in.)

Tamara:	Hi Baby. How's your day been?
Jeff:	Too long to talk about right now. Glad to see you, Tee. Did you get your mother settled in at the hospital?
Tamara:	I sure did. Made sure I met the surgeon who'll be doing the surgery in the morning before I left, too.
Jeff:	I thought you'd already met him?
Tamara:	Me too. But Dr. Price caught the flu and Dr. Joseph, another doctor on staff is taking his place.
Jeff:	Okay, good to know. What's important is she's in good hands.
Tamara:	So true, Jeff. She's getting the best care available.
Jeff:	How are you doing?

(Question gives Tamara pause. She takes a few moments to answer.)

Tamara: Good question. Have been so busy thinking about Mummy and mama, I haven't stopped to think about how I'm doing in a while. First word that comes to mind is blessed.

Jeff: Why is that the first word?

Tamara: Something mama taught me a long time ago. No matter how hard times get, always remember that someone else is always worse off. She also likes to say, 'When troubles get too heavy to carry alone, give them to God knowing that whatever comes, God has your back.' Now that you ask, I'm feeling overwhelmed by blessings...our upcoming wedding...the fact that Mummy's back safe with us and back in school and on the right track where he belongs. I love my work, I have my health...Soon, mama will be back at home and I'll be back in my house. Blessed to have enough in the bank, work I love...Life's good, Jeff. If I could sing, I would.

Jeff: I'm feeling blessed too, Tee. You're the best thing that's ever happened to me. I can't wait to see you walk down the aisle in your dress. Have been getting all of my bachelor's life stuff cleaned out of my apartment too. One thing we can do, once you get back home, is to start looking for the home we'll share together once we're married.

Tamara: Okay, I can't wait baby. We haven't even discussed what area we want to live in yet. Any ideas?

Jeff: I have. Not sure how you'll feel about this, but there's an old four-bedroom house not far from HABO, I'd like us to consider. Everybody in that neighborhood has been there for generations, and it would be nice if we could live where I'm trying to make HABO a permanent and nurturing part of the community. What do you think?

Tamara: I think I haven't lived in the so-called hood for years, but it's where we lived when I was growing up and I believe in what you're trying to do...Let's do it.

(Jeff kisses and hugs her tight.)

Jeff: Thank you, baby...You've surprised the shit out of me. I just knew I was going to have to hit you with every pre-rehearsed counterargument for why you didn't want to do it.

Tamara: I keep telling you, I'm full of surprises and usually good ones.

(*Jeff gets on his knees in front of her and takes her hand.*)

Tamara: Wait, you already asked me to marry you.
Jeff: Tee, you are so crazy...Just want you to know how much I love you, baby...We're going to have an amazing life.

(*They're interrupted by Mummy who gets home an hour before curfew, as Jeff is getting up off his knees.*)

Mummy: Hey, what are you two doing? Jeff, I thought you already asked her to marry you?
Jeff: You ever heard of 'nunya?'

(*Tamara starts to chuckle.*)

Mumia: Nunya? What's that some Swahili?
Jeff: No. It stands for 'none of your business.'
Mumia: Ha, ha. Funny joke. See you two later. Want to play later tonight auntie? No school tomorrow.
Tamara: I'll be ready, nephew. Go upstairs and get washed up and come down and let's have dinner.
Mumia: Okay, see you later, uncle Jeff.

(*Jeff and Tamara look at each other as Mummy heads upstairs.*)

Jeff: Did you hear what he said?
Tamara: Yes, I did. He called you 'uncle' for the first time.
Jeff: Damn. Guess that means he considers me part of the family 'now' huh?
Tamara: Yep. Makes sense too, when you think about it.
Jeff: Meaning what?
Tamara: You saved his life baby and never even raised your voice when we got him back...I don't think he'll ever forget that and neither will I.

(*They have a moment of remembering what happened in silence, then Jeff checks his watch.*)

Jeff:	Oops, have to run Tee, meeting at HABO in about 30 minutes. See you tomorrow.
Tamara:	Okay, let's meet at JoJo's for breakfast.
Jeff:	Time?
Tamara:	8:30?
Jeff:	You got it. Night, Tee.

(He rushes out as Tamara heads to the kitchen to get dinner ready.)

End of Scene

Act III, Scene IV

(Later Friday night after dinner. Tamara and Mumia are seated on the couch talking.)

Tamara:	Will you promise me something Mummy?
Mumia:	If I can. What?
Tamara:	Promise me you'll come home right after school for a couple of weeks after I leave, to look out for mama.
Mumia:	What do you mean?
Tamara:	I mean she's going to need your help while she's healing. The surgery she's having is serious and she's probably going to pretend she doesn't need help when she does.
Mumia:	Alright, Auntie...I promise.
Tamara:	And one more thing.
Mumia:	What?
Tamara:	Get ready to get your butt whooped.

(She starts tickling him.)

Tamara:	Finish putting those leftovers up while I go to the guest room and get the game set up.
Mumia:	Okay, auntie.
Tamara:	And crack the door to let some air in here.
Mumia:	I will.

(She starts to leave, but turns back.)

| Tamara: | And don't forget to close it before you come upstairs. |

(Lights dim as Mumia cracks the front door, then heads for the kitchen to put the food up.)

(A little later. Tamara calls from the guest room in the back of the house.)

Tamara: Come and get this beat down, Mummy.

(Mummy starts to head toward the door to close it, but his phone makes a noise and he pulls it out of his pocket to look as he heads upstairs.)

(Stage darkens to indicate passage of time to 2 o'clock in the morning. A voiceover can be heard.)

Neighbor (vo):   Hello, police? Yes, I meant to call the non-emergency number. Can you send a patrol car over to check my neighbor's house? Her front door is cracked open. My name is Sylvester Brown. Okay, thanks.

(Lights up in spare bedroom. Mummy and Tamara can be seen, deep into the game. Lots of loud shooting sounds and actors should 'improvise' game banter back and forth as a flashlight shines briefly through the back window, followed by the sound of breaking glass.)

(Tamara's been shot by the police officer outside their window, who gave no warning and never checked the front door. Mumia doesn't realize it until she falls over onto his lap.)

Mumia: Auntie!

(Stage to black as a white police officer can be heard.)

Officer (vo):   Shots fired! Shots fired! Need back up. *(Beat)*
News Reporter (vo):   Breaking News: Today after a brief investigation, fired police officer Josh Whitman was arrested and charged with first-degree murder following the shooting of Tamara Johnson in the guest bedroom of her mother's home. According to Whitman's body camera footage, even though the police were called because the front door was open slightly, he never approached the front door.

The End

PART 3

Black/White Double Consciousness

∵

Is There a White Double Consciousness?

A Short Dialogue

Mary E. Weems and Bryant Keith Alexander

Mary E. Weems: All of the white people I've met and developed relationships with have claimed to be either liberals or progressives. In our current socio-political climate, I've been thinking a lot about [author and sociologist W. E. B.] Du Bois' notion of "Double Consciousness" for Black folks and am wondering if some white folks have their own version. Here are a few examples:

A former mentor who has devoted the second half of his career to doing and supporting the kind of work many of us do, and was a major influence in my decision to devote my career to social justice work. I'll never forget the day he told me my imagination-intellect theory had merit and that my work was brilliant. He helped me get my voice and work out in the field—at conference keynotes, publications, etc.—but once he witnessed my "Black Notes" performance at a conference, I contacted him to ask if he would get back to me with the names of colleagues who might be interested in bringing me in to do this piece. While he initially said 'yes,' he never sent me even one. I'd like to think he "forgot," but I followed up enough times to realize: he wasn't going to.

The woman who encouraged me to leave Cleveland. I don't think I would have finished moving forward with pursuing a Ph.D. without her support. When she heard I'd applied to Cleveland State University's Education department, she convinced me to visit UIUC and introduced me to the Head of the Department of Education, who subsequently offered me a graduate fellowship that included a Graduate Assistantship until I earned my Ph.D. Over the years, she has spent the night at my house, I've spent the night at hers, we've broken bread together. We've talked about racism, etc., countless times, and she is the only white woman I've ever called "sister." I thought she knew me, I thought we were kindred spirits. One day, she told me that she saw me as a "dark-skinned Black woman." When I asked why, she said it was because I was always so proud to be Black(?).

Fast forward to yet another conference, the first time we didn't room together. She came to my hotel room so we could walk over to one of the off-campus events together. At the time, I was basking in being able to have a long conversation with two other Black women who I rarely get a chance to spend time with. We were just laughing and talking. When I answered the door, I told her I wasn't ready—the only time I was ever not ready, even though she'd

© MARY E. WEEMS AND BRYANT KEITH ALEXANDER, 2021 | DOI: 10.1163/9789004464858_023 been late several times over the course of our friendship, and offered to meet her at the event. She insisted on waiting, so I invited her in and introduced her. She sat down, and I continued talking while moving around getting my shit together. Suddenly, she got up without a word, left my hotel room door standing wide open...and disappeared for three hours. I kept calling that cell phone that's like an extension of her arm, but it went right to voicemail each time. Worried, I started walking around the hotel to see if I could find her: crickets. Finally, after I've returned to my room, she knocks on my door. I'm pissed, she leaves. Two weeks later, she was still trying to pretend that she didn't know why she did it. One of my friends who witnessed this moment, said, "She alright. She white, that was some white woman shit."

Last, I re-tell an experience a Black male friend and fellow playwright had during an annual residency he taught as part of a remote MFA at a university in Nebraska. One of his white male colleagues had always been welcoming and supportive. Their friendship important enough that he was the best man at my friend's wedding. My friend had been to his home more than once for dinner. Each time, he had the distinct impression that his wife was a racist. Yet, when he suffered two strokes back-to-back during his annual residency with his cohort, and his colleague insisted he stay with them during his recovery, he shared that the woman had been very helpful, preparing his meals, changing his bed clothes, and even helping him bathe.

Is it possible that some so-called liberal, fight-for-social-change white folks have a kind of double consciousness that allows them, acknowledged or not, to retain their racism while working against it?

Bryant Keith Alexander: I am very much in a space, a practiced place of experiencing, knowing, feeling, reflecting upon, and thinking about this idea that "some so-called liberals, fight-for-social-change, white folks who have a kind of double consciousness that allows them, acknowledged or not, to retain [restrain] their racism while working against it?"

There is some slippage or is that seepage?

I am interested in the times in which the construction of "social justice" as a commitment written into the mission of educational institutions becomes a "pale performative," meaning that the mere utterance of the words "social justice" becomes an enactment of making that happen like, "I now pronounce us equal"—when in fact the utterance of that key phrase is not like a bonified priest stating, "I now pronounce you man and wife" (or husband and husband, or wife and wife). The saying of "social justice," or the repetition of a rhetorical trope outside of real actions, does not make real the thing that has been professed and declared. This is not always the case, but I have worked with a range of folks—although not all—who state their commitment to social justice as ritual act yet engage in racist and sexist actions on a daily basis. These include overt actions and micro-aggressions, like silencing dissenting voices of color or ignoring the suggestions of people of color, and then accepting and extolling the same principles and ideas when uttered by someone more socially validated, whether those usual white voices or those acceptable model-minority voices (recognizing the problematics of that construction).

When someone recognizing the injustice, or at least recognizing the grimace on my face, calls out the happening by saying something like, "I appreciated the manner in which Bryant brought out this same notion 10 minutes ago," the irony of the exclusion is placed on the record. And I appreciate that, but it's then swept under the rug without apology, as is the ritual processes of racism and bias to which we (they) profess not to practice.

Or there's the outspoken and sometimes outrageous advocacy of white folks on issues against racism, sexism, lack of diversity, and social injustice that is at times impressive, as in a call for institutional accommodation. But such advocacy always includes self-referential statements that reify their liberal self-interests and deflect perceptions of their own biases by reinforcing their own self-promotion as defensive credit against the notion that they, too, could be possibly racist. The classic defensive tropes include: I dated a Black man. My son or daughter is married to a Black _____. My grandchild is biracial. I voted for _____. My best friend in college was Black. And on and on. Still.

Remind me: What is the difference between slippage and seepage?

- Slippage: the action or process of something slipping or subsiding; the amount or extent of this.
- Seepage: the slow escape of a liquid or gas through porous material or small holes.

Yes, maybe these terms reference what you are suggesting is linked to the double consciousness of white folks, while Du Bois' notion applies to Black folks in a white society and is linked with the challenging injustices found in world systems. In *The Souls of Black Folk*, Du Bois (1989) describes "double consciousness" as follows:

> It is a peculiar sensation, this double-consciousness, this sense of always looking at one's self through the eyes of others, of measuring one's soul by the tape of a world that looks on in amused contempt and pity. One ever feels his two-ness, an American, a Negro; two souls, two thoughts, two unreconciled strivings; two warring ideals in one dark body, whose dogged strength alone keeps it from being torn asunder. The history of the American Negro is the history of this strife—this longing to attain self-conscious manhood, to merge his double self into a better and truer

self. In this merging he wishes neither of the older selves to be lost. He does not wish to Africanize America, for America has too much to teach the world and Africa. He wouldn't bleach his Negro blood in a flood of white Americanism, for he knows that Negro blood has a message for the world. He simply wishes to make it possible for a man to be both a Negro and an American without being cursed and spit upon by his fellows, without having the doors of opportunity closed roughly in his face. (pp. 2–3)

What is the flip side of this statement, to make more palpable your assertion, Mary? Let's try flipping the script a little:

It is a peculiar sensation, this double-consciousness, this sense of always looking at one's self through the eyes of others, of measuring one's soul by the tape of a world that looks on in amused contempt and pity. One ever feels his OR HER two-ness, an American, *a LIBERAL* WHITE and/or LIBERAL CAUCASOID; two souls, two thoughts, two unreconciled strivings; two warring ideals in one LITE body, whose dogged strength is focused on MAINTAINING ITS SUPERIOR SOCIAL POSITION WITHOUT A CRITIQUE OF BEING RACIST. The history of the MODERN American WHITE and/or CAUCASOID is the history of this strife—this longing to RETAIN self-conscious SUPERIORITY, WHILE NOT CANCELLING THE MECHANISM OF SUSTAINING THE SOCIAL PRIVILEGES OF WHITENESS to merge AND CONCEAL this double self into a SUSTAINED SENSE OF SELF WITHOUT CRITIQUE. In this merging he OR SHE wishes neither of the older selves to be lost. He OR SHE does not wish to KEEP AMERICA WHITE, BUT "TO MAKE AMERICA GREAT AGAIN," for America has too much to teach the world and Africa. He OR SHE wouldn't DENY THEIR WHITE and/or CAUCASOID blood in a flood of DEMOCRATIC/EQUAL Americanism, for he OR SHE knows that WHITE and/or CAUCASOID blood has a message for the world. He OR SHE simply wishes to make it possible TO MAINTAIN THEIR SUPERIOR, NOW LIBERAL IDENTITY to be both WHITE and or CAUCASOID and LIBERAL—WITH ALL THE PRIVILEGES THEREIN without being cursed and spit upon FOR THE OVERT PERFORMANCES OF LIBERALNESS, without having the doors of WHITE PRIVILEGE BEING closed roughly in his OR HER face.

So, Mary, in response to your question: "Is it possible that some so-called liberals, fight-for-social-change white folks have a kind of double consciousness that allows them, acknowledged or not, to retain their racism while working against it?" Well, what do you think?

Study Questions, Prompts, and Probes

Bryant Keith Alexander

This book privileges lived experience, which is at the foundation of all human existence. As you further engage our work through the following questions, prompts, and probes, it's important to remain open to parts of the book that either connect or disconnect to your life, including critically reflecting upon why, as part of your journey toward deconstructing racism.

Part 1: Sounds of Blackness

- How do you articulate the unifying theme of the section "Sounds of Blackness?"
- What are the references to *sound* that might reference *blackness*?
- How do you define "blackness," less as a racial concept and more from a cultural and performative perspective? What does that mean? What is the relationship between race and culture?
- What ties all of these pieces together under this theme?
- Can you provide more examples in the Black historical songbook that you might define as songs of or in protest or prayer? What is a "song of protest?" Choose a song that you have identified as a "song of protest" and do a line-by-line lyrical analysis that shows the evidence of why you believe it to be a song of, as, and/or in protest? What is it protesting in favor of or against?
- How do you understand the opening frame of the collection "Black Notes?" How would you outline the historical timeline that Weems travels in this performative piece?
- What is the function or purpose of performance in the two stage plays: "Still Hanging" and "Black Notes"? What is "performance?" How would you outline the arguments of these performance texts? What is an argument?
- How do you read the "interludes" throughout this project? Do they stand as individual pieces? Or does their purpose merely reflect and foreshadow what has preceded and what follows?
- In "Let the People see what they did to my Son," what does the mother want "the People" to see? Who are "the People?" What is the tension in this mother's position in this situation?
- In "Wendy's, Me, and Rayshard Brooks," what is the author's positionality in the piece? Where and how does the author locate himself in relation to

© BRYANT KEITH ALEXANDER, 2021 | DOI: 10.1163/9789004464858_024

"Wendy's," his childhood memory, and the public news of Rayshard Brook's murder?

– Do you know the historical reference of the phrase, "Where's the Beef?" What is the author playing on by using that phrase in this context? What is "the beef" in this context? What is the answer to the question, "Where is the beef?" What do you make of the, "Where's the Beef?" piece following "Wendy's, Me, and Rayshard"? Do a comparative analysis between the two pieces.

– Do you know how many unarmed Black men have been killed by police in the U.S.? Research the statistics relative to the time that you are engaging this assignment.

– In "Three Meditations on Prayer and Particularity," what is the author trying to get at in your opinion? What is the role of church or religion in the Black community as you understand it? The author speaks to notions of being both "particular and plural." What does that mean relative to your understanding of race and gender? How do you understand the notion of intersectionality? How does intersectionality play out in your own lived experience?

– There are multiple references to mothers in this volume. List a few and analyze their significance in context.

– In "Three Conversations," which piece are you most attracted to as a reflection of truth? Which piece are you most alarmed by? Which character is most like you? Do you recognize these characters? Choose one piece—"A Conversation in an Elevator," "A Conversation in a Bus Stop," or "A Conversation at a Black Lives Matter March"—and re-write the script with what you believe is a more emancipatory dialogue or ending. What does the notion of "emancipatory dialogue" mean to you? You have been offered three scenes with three combinations of characters in dialogue. What scene is missing? Who are the characters? Where are they located? What brings them together? What happens at the end?

– In "A Conversation at a Black Lives Matter March," what do these two individuals have in common? What is the same and what is different besides their age and race?

– Is this conversation too civil given the turbulence and/or context of their encounter? Why or why not?

– How might understanding John's immigration story be compared to Africans being transported to this country? What is the same and what is different?

– With respect to John's query, what is the difference in these "coming to America stories" that require African Americans to hold on to the politics of "skin color" relative to identity and Americanness?

– What is it in John and DaRonda that allows this conversation to continue, and to end in this fashion?
– What is the tension between converting the phrase "Black Lives Matter" to "All Lives Matter" in this particular context?
– What is the depth of meaning in DaRonda's statement: "The rest of my life wouldn't be enough time to explain it to you"?
– At the end of the scene, when DaRonda leans in for a quick hug, theorize the hug. What does that hug symbolize to you?
– "Eat Fresh" and "Not a Fan Letter" both focus on the case of Jussie Smollett. Have you researched that case? What is your opinion of it? Why do you think the authors included these pieces focused on this person? Are there other cases in the public news that speak to so-called race-baiting or deception? How would you define "race baiting"? Do you know the case of Rachel Dolezal? Research the case of Rachel Dolezal through the frame of racial performance and passing. Define the terms "racial performance," "cultural performance," and "passing" as you outline your understanding. Is this a case of "racial performance?"

Part 2: Bodies on the Line

– How do you articulate the unifying theme of the section "Bodies on the Line?"
– What does it mean to "put your body on the line," versus "have your body on the line?"
– Have you studied the history of lynching in America? What was lynching used for in the politics of race? Research the statistics.
– What does the expression "crack the door for some air" mean to you? How is the phrase used in the construct of this play?
– Do you know how many unarmed Black women and women of color have been killed by police in America? Research the statistics.
– The pieces "Attached?" and "Still Hanging" are explicitly about the increase of hanging deaths—or lynchings—of Black people in 2019 and 2020. How do you make sense of the resurgence of lynching? How do you make sense of the increase of lynching alongside the rise of Black Lives Matter? Regardless of your politics, is there a correlation between the increase in lynchings in American and a Donald J. Trump presidency?

Part 3: Is There a White Double Consciousness? (A Dialogue)

- How do you articulate the unifying theme of the section "Is There a White Double Consciousness?"
- How do you make sense of this dialogue?
- What is your understanding of the abiding construct of "double consciousness?"
- What is your understanding of the concept of "flipping the script?"
- Do you think that this flip works, relative to your understanding of social politics, cultural politics, and racial politics in America? What do those terms mean to you?

Notes for Teachers, Faculty, and Facilitators on Establishing a Learning Community

Mary E. Weems

What follows is a method developed as part of the praxis component of my Imagination-Intellect Theory and practiced in my classrooms and workshops for over a decade. It's designed to help groups come together as a safe learning community and/or collective grounded in mutual respect, reciprocal learning, caring, and sharing with each other.

Day One

As the students or participants enter, welcome them, and ask them to draw numbers designed to randomly divide them into small groups of about five people. ("Number the slips of paper based on the number of course or workshop registrations; for example, if there are 25 participants, there should be five sets of paper slips numbered 1 through 5.)

Invite students to sit with their group members.

Share an overview of the course or workshop, including the kind of safe space you need to create as a learning community or collective where:

- Each facilitator and participant is invited to consciously acknowledge the importance of his, her, or their reflexivity, remaining critically self-reflective about the biases, beliefs, and perceptions which inform how they see and operate in the world as, in this case, they pertain to race.
- Participants consciously acknowledge his, her, or their positionality in society. For example: Black, hetero, female from a poor, working-class background.
- Each person's opinion is to be respected and not judged.
- Learning is reciprocal, or a two-way process. Teachers, faculty members, and facilitators learn from the students, and the students learn from the facilitator(s) and from fellow participants.
- Caring about and respecting each other is understood to be a necessary part of deconstructing racism or dealing with any difficult social issue.

- Participants share with one other from lived experience, including being as honest as possible and remaining consciously open to receiving what other group members will share without doubting what they share is their truth.

Ask if anyone has any questions or comments. If yes, discuss.

Ice Breaker:

- Ask everyone to stand.
- Using a clock, ask them to begin introducing themselves in pairs, asking one other their names, one thing they love about themselves, and the story of the last time they laughed, until the facilitator says, "Time."
- At the end of 10 to 15 minutes, end the session by asking everyone to stop where they are, pair off with someone they've met during the exercise, and introduce each other to the entire group.
- Next, ask the students to return to their original groups and provide about 10 to 15 minutes for the group members to continue getting to know one other while the facilitator moves from one group to the next listening and/or commenting. Ask the group for comments about the experience.
- Ask each group to select a group leader who will be responsible for moderating group discussions and keeping the group on-task.
- Pass out the course syllabus and/or workshop overview and discuss.
- Pass out the "Bibliography on Racism" and "Bibliography on Anti-Racism" designed for further study and deconstruction work.

Day Two

Each teacher, faculty member, or facilitator should remain an active participant in the learning community/collective for the duration of the course or workshop. Continue to share from your lived experience, and reinforce the fact that the perspectives of all members of the learning community are welcome.

Ice Breaker:

Once students or participants are seated with their groups, ask each to share either the real story of their name or a brief story from their family history. (Duration: 10 to 15 minutes.)

Day Three

Once students or participants are seated with their groups, ask everyone to discuss within their groups when they first became aware that there are different races. (Duration: 10 to 15 minutes.)

After the allotted time has passed, ask for one volunteer from each group to share his, her, or their story.

Note: I found that after the first three sessions with each class or workshop group, we had spent enough time with introductory activities and discussions to establish a safe space for our journey. For all remaining classes and sessions, we spent the entire time discussing the readings and engaging in critical self-reflection.

Bibliography and Further Reading

Alexander, B. K. (2006). *Performing black masculinity: Race, culture, and queer identity.* Altamira Press.

Alexander, B. K. (2020, June 11). *gogputyourselfonyourknees.* Loyola Marymount University, Manresa Moments Series. https://mission.lmu.edu/respondingtoourcrisis/manresamoments/

Alexander, B. K. (2020, June 17). On social justice, Black Lives Matter and the power of prayer. *Diverse: Issues in Higher Education.* https://diverseeducation.com/article/181085/

Alexander, B. K. (2021). Dense particularities: Race, spirituality, and queer/quare intersectionalities. In M. N. Goins, J. McAlister, & K. A. Alexander (Eds.), *The Routledge international handbook of communication and gender.* Routledge Press.

Alexander, B. K., & Weems, M. E. (Eds.). (2017). Special issue: Terrorism and hate in Orlando, America: Poetic and performative responses. *Qualitative Inquiry, 23*(7), 483–571.

Arnold, A. (2019, April 23). A complete timeline of the Jussie Smollett case. *New York Magazine: The Cut.* https://www.thecut.com/2019/04/a-complete-timeline-of-the-jussie-smollett-case.html.

BBC News. (2018, May 2). Kanye West suggests African-American slavery was 'a choice.' https://www.bbc.com/news/world-us-canada-43970903

Berman, M., & Farzan, A. N. (2018, July 30). Minneapolis police officers won't be charged for fatally shooting Thurman Blevins. *Washington Post.* https://www.washingtonpost.com/news/morning-mix/wp/2018/07/30/thurman-blevins-shooting-graphic-body-cam-footage-shows-fleeing-black-man-killed-by-minneapolis-police-who-say-he-was-armed/?noredirect=on&utm_term-=8ddi596ced8

Carìssimo, J., & McNamara, A. (2020, June 14). Atlanta police officer fired after fatally shooting black man Rayshard Brooks. *CBS News.* https://www.cbsnews.com/news/rayshard-brooks-atlanta-killed-by-police-protests/

CBS News. (2018, May 14). Woman's body found hanging from tree outside Walmart in Georgia. https://www.cbsnews.com/news/south-fulton-georgia-woman-body-hanging-tree-outside-walmart-police-say/

Certeau, M. (1984). *The practice of everyday life.* University of California Press.

Conquergood, D. (2002). Performance studies: Interventions and radical research. *The Drama Reviews, 46*(2), 152.

Denisoff, R. S. (1968). Protest movements: Class consciousness and the propaganda song. *Sociological Quarterly, 9*(2), 229–230.

Dolan, J. (2008). *Utopia in performance: Finding hope at the theater.* University of Michigan Press.

Earle, G. (2019, January 31). 'Trump condemns 'horrible' attack that left 'Empire' actor Jussie Smollett bloodied by perpetrators who allegedly yelled 'MAGA country.' *Daily Mail Online.* https://www.dailymail.co.uk/news/article-6654489/Trump-condemns-horrible-attack-Empire-actor-Jussie-Smollett.html

Empire (2015 TV series). (n.d.). In *Wikipedia.* https://en.wikipedia.org/wiki/Empire_(2015_TV_series)

Ferguson unrest. (n.d.). In *Wikipedia.* https://en.wikipedia.org/wiki/Ferguson_unrest

Filewod, A. (2001). Coalitions of resistance: Ground zero's community mobilization. In *Performing democracy: International perspectives on urban community-based performance* (pp. 89–103). University of Michigan Press.

Fuist, T. N. (2014). The dramatization of beliefs, values, and allegiances: Ideological performances among social movement groups and religious organizations. *Social Movement Studies, 13*(4), 427–442.

Fuoss, K. (1997). *Striking performances/performing strikes.* University of Mississippi.

Fuoss, K. W. (1999). Lynching performances, theatres of violence. *Text and Performance Quarterly, 19*(1), 1–37.

Hands up, don't shoot. (n.d.). In *Wikipedia.* https://en.wikipedia.org/wiki/Hands_up,_don%27t_shoot

Harris, A., & Holman, S. (2018). Activist affect. *Qualitative Inquiry.* doi.org/10.1177/1077800753

Hopkins, M. F. (1981). From page to stage: The burden of proof. *Southern Speech Communication Journal, 47*(1), 1–9.

Hughes, L. (n.d.). *Harlem.* Poetry Foundation. https://www.poetryfoundation.org/poems/46548/harlem

Jarve, J. (2020, June 17). Atlanta police officer who shot Rayshard Brooks charged with murder. *Los Angeles Times.* https://www.latimes.com/world-nation/story/2020-06-17/atlanta-police-officer-who-shot-rayshard-brooks-charged?utm_source=sfmc_100035&utm_medium=email&utm_campaign=News+Alert%3a+Atlanta+police+officer+who+shot+Rayshard+Brooks+charged++0000001172-c3df-deff-a7fe-ebff7a&utm_term=https%3a%2f%2fwww.latimes.com%2fworld-nation%2fstory%2f2020-06-17%2fatlanta-police-officer-who-shot-rayshard-brooks-charged&utm_id=845o&sfmc_id=44o712

Johnson, E. P. (2003). Strange Fruit: A performance about identity politics. *TDR, 47*(2), 88–116.

Johnson, E. P. (2012). From page to stage: The making of sweet tea. *Text and Performance Quarterly, 32*(2), 248–253.

Jones, J. L. (1997). "Sista Docta?": Performance as critique of the academy. *TDR, 41*(2), 51–67.

King, M. J. (1963, August 28). "I have a dream" Speech. Stanford University Martin Luther King, Jr. Research and Education Institute. https://kinginstitute.stanford.edu/king-papers/documents/i-have-dream-address-delivered-march-washington-jobs-and-freedom

Morality plays. (n.d.). In *Wikipedia*. https://en.wikipedia.org/wiki/Morality_play

Now this. Groundhog day for a Black man: shows danger Black men in America face. (n.d.). YouTube. https://www.youtube.com/watch?v=tbTrSfyJcJA

O'Kane, C. (2020, June 8). Say their names: The list of people injured or killed in offi-cer-involved incidents is still growing. *CBS News*. https://www.cbsnews.com/news/say-their-names-list-people-injured-killed-police-officer-involved-incidents/

Oluo, I. (2018). *So you want to talk about race*. Seal Press.

Pineau, E. L. (2002). Critical performative pedagogy: Fleshing out the politics of libera-tory education. In N. Stucky & C. Wimmer (Eds.), *Teaching performance studies* (pp. 41–54). Southern Illinois University Press.

Platt, G. M., & Williams, R. H. (2002). Ideological language and social movement mobi-lization: A sociolinguistic analysis of segregationists' ideologies. *Sociological Theory*, 20, 336.

Reeve, E. (2017, August 14). Charlottesville: Race and terror. *VICE News Tonight*. https://video.vice.com/en_us/video/charlottesville-race-and-terror-vice-news-tonight-on-hbo/599z1b1d2f8d32d808pd8ddfbc

Shooting of Trayvon Martin. (n.d.). In *Wikipedia*. https://en.wikipedia.org/wiki/Shooting_of_Trayvon_Martin

Snapes L. (2019, January 2). Kanye West pledges to perform in Maga hat, and reaffirms presidential ambitions. *The Guardian*. https://www.theguardian.com/music/2019/jan/02/kanye-west-pledges-to-perform-in-maga-hat-reaffirms-hat-presidential-ambitions

Taibbi, M. (2017). *I can't breathe: The killing that started a movement*. Spiegel & Grau. https://books.google.com/books/about/I_Can_t_Breathe.html?id=zQ_BQAACAAJ&hl=en

The case of the Jena Six. (n.d.). In *Wikipedia*. https://www.democracynow.org/2007/7/10/the_case_of_the_jena_six

Turner, V. (1982). *From ritual to theatre*. PAJ Publications.

Vives, R. (2020, June 19). Family says Malcolm Harsch, Black man found hanging from tree, died by apparent suicide. *Los Angeles Times*. https://www.latimes.com/california/story/2020-06-19/malcolm-harsch-committed-harsch-suicide-family?utm_source=sfmc_10003509&utm_medium=email&utm_campaign=News+Alert%3a+Family+says+Malcolm+Harsch+died+by+apparent+suicide+in+Victorville++00000172-c10b-d69c-a9bb-d73fa0000172?utm_term=https%3a%2f%2fwww.latimes.com%2fcalifornia%2fstory%2f2020-06-19%2fmalcolm-harsch-committed-suicide-family&utm_id=8679&sfmc_id=440712

Weems, M. E. (2003). *Public education and the imagination-intellect*. Peter Lang Inc.

Weems, M. E. (2006). Colorblind. *XCP: Cross Cultural Poetics*, 15/16, 190.

Young, H. (2010). *Embodying Black experience: Stillness, critical memory, and the Black body*. The University of Michigan Press.

Further Reading on Racism

Allen, J. (2004). *Without sanctuary*. www.withoutsanctuary.org

Allen, J. (2004). *Without sanctuary: Lynching photography in America* (1st ed.). Twin Palms Publishers.

Baldwin, J. (1985). *The price of the ticket: Collected nonfiction 1948–1985* (1st ed.). St. Martin's Press.

Baldwin, J. (1985). Stranger in the village. In *The price of the ticket: Collected nonfiction 1948–1985* (pp. 79–90). St. Martin's Press.

Balkin, J. M. (2002). *What "Brown v. Board of Education" should have said* (1st paperback ed.). New York University Press.

Barndt, J. R. (1991). *Dismantling racism: The continuing challenge to White America*. Augsburg Fortress.

Bell, D. A. (1980). *Race, racism, and American law* (2nd ed.). Little, Brown and Company.

Bell, D. A. (1992). *Faces at the bottom of the well: The permanence of racism*. Basic Books.

Black Issues in Higher Education (Anderson, J., & Byrne, D. N., Eds.). (2004). *The unfinished agenda of Brown v. Board of Education*. John Wiley & Sons.

Boyd, H. (Ed.) (2002). *Race and resistance: African Americans in the 21st century*. South End Press.

Branch, T. (1988). *Parting the waters: America in the King years 1954–1963*. Simon & Schuster Paperbacks.

Branch, T. (1988). Preface. In *Parting the waters: America in the King years 1954–1963* (pp. xi–xii). Simon & Schuster Paperback.

Branch, T. (1999). *Pillar of fire: America in the King years 1963–1965* (1st ed.) Touchstone Simon & Schuster.

Brooks, R. L. (1992). *Rethinking the American race problem* (1st paperback printing ed.). University of California Press.

Bulmer, M., & Solomos, J. (Eds.). (1999). *Racism*. Oxford University Press.

Chafe, W. H., Gavins, R., & Korstad, R. (Eds.). (2001). *Remembering Jim Crow: African Americans tell about life in the segregated south*. The New Press.

Cimbala, P. A., & Himmelberg, R. F. (Eds.). (1996). *Historians & race: Autobiography and the writing of history*. Indiana University Press.

Davidson, D. (1973). The furious passage of the Black graduate student. In J. A. Ladner (Ed.), *The death of White sociology: Essays on race and culture* (pp. 23–51). Black Classic Press.

Davis, A. Y. (1990). *Women, race & class* (First Vintage Books ed.). Vintage Books.

Davis, A. Y. (1990). *Women, culture, & politics* (First Vintage Books ed.). Vintage Books.

de Tocqueville, A. (1994). *Democracy in America*. Alfred A. Knopf, Inc. (Original work published 1835)

de Tocqueville, A. (1994). The present and probable future conditions of the three races that inhabit the territory of the United States (Chapter XVIII). In *Democracy in America* (Vol. 1, pp. 331–434). Alfred Knopf, Inc. (Original work published 1835)

Delgado, R., & Stefanic, J. (2001). *Critical race theory: An introduction*. New York University Press.

Du Bois, W. E. B. (1989). *The souls of Black folk*. Penguin Books. (Original work published 1903)

Du Bois, W. E. B. (1992). *Black reconstruction in America: 1860–1880*. Atheneum. (Original work published 1935)

Early, G. (Ed.). (1994). *Lure and loathing: Essays on race, identity, and the ambivalence of assimilation*. The Penguin Group.

Eze, E. C. (Ed.). (1997). *Race and enlightenment: A reader*. Blackwell Publishers.

Fanon, F. (1963). *The wretched of the earth* (reprint ed.). Grove Press.

hooks, b. (1998). Representations of Whiteness in the Black imagination. In D. R. Roediger (Ed.), *Black on White: Black writers on what it means to be White* (pp. 38–53). Schocken Books.

Hord, F. L., & Lee, J. S. (Eds.). (1995). *I am because we are: Readings in Black philosophy*. University of Massachusetts Press.

Jackson, C. E., & Tolbert, F. J. (Eds.). (1989). *Race and culture in America: Readings in racial and ethnic relations* (3rd ed.). Burgess International Group.

Jefferson, T. (1982). *Notes on the State of Virginia: Edited and with an introduction & notes by William Peden*. University of North Carolina Press.

Jefferson, T. (1982). Query XIV: Laws. In W. Peden (Ed.), *Notes on the State of Virginia: Edited and with an introduction & notes by William Peden* (pp. 130–149). University of North Carolina Press.

Jensen, R. (2005). *The heart of Whiteness: Confronting race, racism and White privilege*. City Lights Books.

Ladner, J. A. (Ed.). (1998). *The death of White sociology: Essays on race and culture* (2nd ed.). Palgrave.

Matsuda, M. J., Lawrence, C. R. I., Delgado, R., & Crenshaw Williams, K. (1993). *Words that wound: Critical race theory, assaultive speech, and the First Amendment*. Westview Press.

McCarthy, C., & Crichlow, W. (Eds.). (1993). *Race, identity, and representation in education*. Routledge.

Memmi, A. (1991). *The colonizer and the colonized* (expanded ed.). Beacon Press. (Original work published 1965)

Myrdal, G. (1975). *An American dilemma: The Negro problem and modern democracy.* Pantheon. (Original work published 1944)

Omi, M., & Winant, H. (1994). *Racial formation in the United States: From the 1960s to the 1990s* (2nd ed.). Routledge.

Outlaw, L. T. (1996). *On race and philosophy.* Routledge.

Patterson, J. T. (2001). *Brown vs. Board of Education: A civil rights milestone and its troubled legacy.* Oxford University Press.

Patterson, J. T. (2001). Race and schools before Brown (Chapter One). In *Brown v. Board of Education: A civil rights milestone and its troubled legacy* (pp. 1–20). Oxford University Press.

Roediger, D. R. (Ed.). (1998). *Black on White: Black writers on what it means to be White.* Schocken.

Sefa-Dei, G. J. (1996). *Anti-racism education: Theory & practice.* Fernwood Publishers.

Sitkoff, H. (1993). *The struggle for Black equality: 1954–1992* (revised ed.). Hill and Wang.

Steinhorn, L., & Diggs-Brown, B. (1999). *By the color of our skin: The illusion of integration and the reality of race* (1st ed.). Dutton/Penguin.

Tatum, B. D. (1997). *"Why are all the Black kids sitting together in the cafeteria?" and other conversations about race* (1st ed.). Basic Books.

West, C. (1993). *Race matters.* Beacon Press.

Wise, T. (2005). *White like me: Reflections on race from a privileged son.* Soft Skull Press.

Wolfenstein, E. V. (1993). Chapter One: The problem. In *The victims of democracy: Malcolm X and the Black revolution* (2nd printing ed., pp. 1–41). Guilford Press. (Original work published 1981)

Wolfenstein, E. V. (1993). *The victims of democracy: Malcolm X and the Black revolution* (2nd printing ed.). Guilford Press. (Original work published 1981)

Woodson, C. G. (1977). *Miseducation of the Negro.* AMS Press. (Original work published 1933)

X, Malcolm & Haley, A. (1999). *The autobiography of Malcolm X as told to Alex Haley* (new foreword by Attallah Shabazz ed.). Balantine Books. (Original work published 1964)

Further Reading on Anti-Racism

Adams, M. (Ed.). (2010). *Reading for diversity and social justice.* Routledge.

Alexander, B. K. (2012). *The performative sustainability of race: Reflections on Black culture and the politics of identity.* Peter Lang.

Alexander, M. (2012). *The new Jim Crow: Mass incarceration in the age of colorblindness* (revised ed.). The New Press.

Arnold, J. (2020). *Raising our hands: How white women can stop avoiding hard conver-sations, start accepting responsibility, and find our place on the frontlines*. BanBella Books Inc.

Barndt, J. (1991). *Dismantling racism: The continuing challenge to White America*. Augs-burg.

Bartoletti, S. C. (2010). *They called themselves the K.K.K.: The birth of an American ter-rorist group*. Houghton Mifflin Harcourt.

Bell, L. A. (2010). *Storytelling for social justice: Connecting narrative and the arts in anti-racist teaching*. Routledge.

Blaine, B. E. (2013). *Understanding the psychology of diversity*. Sage.

Bonnett, A. (2005). *Anti-racism*. Routledge.

Bowser, B. P. (1995). *Racism and anti-racism in world perspective*. Sage.

Coates, T. N. (2015). *Between the world and me*. Spiegel & Grau.

Cooper, B. (2018). *Eloquent rage: A Black feminist discovers her superpower*. Picador.

Connelly, K. (2020). *Good white racist? Confronting your role in racial injustice*. West-minster John Knox Press.

Derman-Sparks, L., & Phillips, C. B. (1997). *Teaching/learning anti-racism*. Teachers College Press.

DiAngelo, R. J. (2018). *White fragility: Why it's so hard for White people to talk about rac-ism*. Beacon Press.

Dudziak, M. L. (2000). *Cold War civil rights: Race and the image of American democracy*. Princeton University Press.

Eberhardt, J. L. (2020). *Biased: Uncovering the hidden prejudice that shapes what we see, think, and do*. Penguin Random House.

Fidel, K. (2020). *The antiracist: How to start the conversation about race and take action*. Skyhorse Publishing.

Fine, M. (2004). *Off white: Readings on power, privilege, and resistance*. Routledge.

Fitzgerald, A. (2020). *Antiracism and universal design for learning*. CAST, Inc.

Hughey, M. (2012). *White bound: Nationalists, antiracists, and the shared meaning of race*. Stanford University Press.

Jewell, T., & Durand, A. (2020). *This book is anti-racist: 20 lessons on how to wake up, take action, and do the work*. The Quarto Group.

Kailin, J. (2002). *Antiracist education: From theory to practice*. Rowman & Littlefield.

Kendi, I. X. (2016). *Stamped from the beginning: The definitive history of racist ideas in America*. Nation Books.

Kendi, I. X. (2019). *How to be an antiracist*. Random House Publishing Group.

Karumanchery, L. (Ed.). (2005). *Engaging equity: New perspectives on anti-racist educa-tion*. Detselig Enterprises.

Katz, J. H. (2003). *White awareness: Handbook for anti-racism training*. University of Oklahoma Press.

Kivel, P. (2002). *Uprooting racism: How white people can work for racial justice*. New Society Publishers.

Loewen, J. (1996). *Lies my teacher told: Everything your American history textbook got wrong*. Touchstone.

Lorde, A. (2007). *Sister outsider: Essays & speeches by Audre Lorde*. Crossing Press.

Meacham, J., & Lewis, J. (2020). *His truth is marching on: John Lewis and the power of hope*. Penguin Random House.

Michael, A. (2015). *Raising race questions: Whiteness and inquiry in education*. Teachers College Press.

Muhammad, K. G. (2011). *The condemnation of Blackness: Race, crime, and the making of modern urban America*. Harvard University Press.

Owens, L. R. (2020). *Love and rage: The path of liberation through anger*. North Atlantic Books.

Parker, R., & Chambers, P. S. (2005). *The anti-racist cookbook: A recipe guide for conversations about race that goes beyond covered dishes and "Kum-Bah-Ya."* Crandall, Dostie, & Douglass Books, Inc.

Roberts, D. (2011). *Fatal invention: How science, politics, and big business re-create race in the twenty-first century*. New Press.

Rothstein, R. (2017). *The color of law: A forgotten history of how our government segregated America*. Liveright Publishing Corporation.

Rothenberg, P. S. (2004). *White privilege: Essential readings on the other side of racism*. Worth Publishers.

Saad, L., & DiAngelo, R. (2020). *Me and white supremacy: Combat racism, change the world, and become a good ancestor*. Sourcebooks.

Sensoy, Ö. (2012). *Is everyone really equal? An introduction to key concepts in social justice education*. Teachers College Press.

Simien, J. (Producer & Director). (2014). *Dear white people* [Motion picture]. Code Red Films.

Smedley, A. (1999). *Race in North America: origin and evolution of a worldview*. Westview Press.

Smith, C. (2017). *The cost of privilege: Taking on the system of white supremacy and racism*. Camino Press.

Tatum, B. (1997). *Why are all the Black kids sitting together in the cafeteria? And other conversations about race*. Basic Books.

Theoharis, J. (2018). *More beautiful and terrible history: The uses and misuses of civil rights story*. Beacon Press.

Tochluk, S. (2008). *Witnessing whiteness: First steps toward an antiracist practice and culture*. Rowman & Littlefield Education.

Twine, F. (2000). *Racing research, researching race: Methodological dilemmas in critical race studies*. New York University Press.

Weems, M. E. (2015). *Blackeyed: Plays and monologues.* Sense Publishers.

White, D. (1999). *Too heavy a load: Black women in defense of themselves, 1894–1994.* W.W. Norton.

Wilkerson, I. (2020). *Caste: The origins of our discontent.* Penguin Random House.

Wise, T. (2008). *Speaking treason fluently: Anti-racist reflections from an angry white male.* Soft Skull Press.

Wise, T. J. (2010). *Colorblind: The rise of post-racial politics and the retreat from racial equity.* City Lights Books.

Wise, T. (2011). *White like me: Reflections on race from a privileged son.* Soft Skull Press.

Wright, W. D. (1998). *Racism matters.* Greenwood Publishing Group.

Zinn, H. (2001). *A people's history of the United States: 1492–present.* Harper.